Where Thoughts and Stories End

Verses on Eternal Truth

Solomon Katz

Copyright © 2019 by Solomon Katz
solomonkatz.com
All Rights Reserved

ISBN 13: 9780989111232
ISBN 10: 0989111237
Library of Congress Control Number: 2019905558
Deeper Currents Press
Harvard, Massachusetts

Table of Contents

Preface: Truth and Beauty i
1. Frontispiece: Truth and Beauty (via Dogs) 1
2. The God Hypothesis 5
3. Verses on Stillness 29
4. Chicken Thoughts 33
5. Metaphysical Chicken Thoughts 35
6. Verses on Philosophy 53
7. Belief System Chicken Thoughts 57
8. Personal Chicken Thoughts 97
9. Verses on Psychology 109
10. Verses on Truth 131
11. Verses on Beauty 149
References 165
About the Author 167

*for all my beloved daughters and sons
and the generations that will follow*

*God,
can never be,
distant,
absent,
or other.*

As a ray of light shined through a prism,
diffracts into a spectrum of color,
the Eternal Light,
when shined through the body,
diffracts into the spectrum of the five senses,
and world perception.

Preface: Truth and Beauty

When I was a student in college, I thought I might like to someday become a college professor. I was studying philosophy, was enamored with ideas, and thought no life could be better than a life immersed in ideas. Like my favorite philosophers at the time - the existentialists mostly - I hoped to write literary philosophy: profound ideas but expressed beautifully, in literary fashion. A few years ago I wrote my first book, "Beauty as a State of Being" (which I will refer to going forward as BSB). In the preface to BSB, while laying out my intentions for the book, I stated that I was trying to write both a manual of mind and a work of art. I was trying to write literary philosophy: ideas regarding a theory of mind, expressed beautifully as a work of art.

In BSB I refer to a notion from the Kabbalah, the system of Jewish mysticism. According to this creation model, the One Infinite Consciousness ("Ein Soph" in Hebrew - Without End - Endlessness) descends into manifestation through the process of creation, forming first very rarefied and then denser worlds like our own, where the Endless Source is heavily veiled. In other words, Endlessness veils itself in layer after layer of attributes and, as layers are added on, the brilliance of the Endless Source becomes more veiled and so less apparent. (But even in our mess of a world, for those who have eyes to see, Endlessness is hiding in plain sight; there is never anything other than Endlessness)! So Endlessness, the One Source, splits into the most rarefied division - two-ness - and then continues to diversify. This is like cellular division in a zygote, which splits from one cell into two cells, then into four cells, then into millions of cells as the zygote develops. Some believe that the primary split of the One, the first split of the One into two, is the split into the principles of truth and beauty, the male and female principles, the most rarefied of the Platonic ideas, once Oneness decides to make Something of itself.

(I can hear a Jewish mother saying to God, "It's about time you made something of yourself)!

In attempting to write literary philosophy, I am paying homage to these two principles. Philosophy, the contemplation of ideas, is the quest for truth. Literature, the artistic aspiration, is the worship of beauty. In this writing I am hoping to incorporate these two principles: the contemplation of truth and the worship of beauty.

In the preface to BSB I also state that the great sage, Ramana Maharshi - like light from a lighthouse penetrating a fog, guiding the way - is my beacon. According to Ramana, and consistent with Indian and many other spiritual traditions, there are two paths to the source: the path of inquiry and the path of surrender. But these two paths similarly pay homage to our two principles as inquiry seeks liberating truth, and surrender adores and bows before beauty. By holding either to the beacon of truth or to the beacon of beauty, you retrace your steps, ascend, find your way out of the fog of manifestation, back to the source of light, the Eternal Light, tracing the beacon back to the lighthouse, the light source prior to its refraction into the two primary faces of truth and beauty.

"Beauty as a State of Being," as the title indicates, leans toward beauty. This book will lean toward truth. But hopefully you will find here literary philosophy - ideas expressed beautifully - truth and beauty - and your soul will rejoice.

If I were now a college professor, I would teach a class in spiritual enlightenment. I would begin with basics and progress toward more advanced expressions of enlightenment. During the course I would build a vocabulary of ideas. By the end of the course, a vocabulary and the body of knowledge it represents would be mastered. I suppose this is the process of mastering any body of knowledge.

I will not assume that present readers have read BSB. I will therefore begin the narrative by referencing some of the ideas first introduced in BSB, which I will build upon. For those who have read BSB, I apologize for any repetition. But repetition is actually an important part of spiritual learning. Truth must be heard over and over again to sink in fully. Suzuki Roshi once said that Zen was like walking in a fog: it takes a while to get wet but eventually you are completely soaked. Spiritual transformation is a process of getting soaked in truth, hearing the teaching again and again, until falsehood - the habit of the false mind - is undone, the false mind capitulates, and the radiant heart of truth emerges - in all its joy and splendor.

And now on towards truth and beauty!

1. Frontispiece: Truth and Beauty (via Dogs)

Dog is God spelled backwards and I think that is no coincidence. When I meditate with my gorgeous Sheltie, Henry, as a focus, I feel love in all directions, coming from Henry, moving towards Henry, Henry an incarnation of love, a doorway to open heartedness, my eyes filling as my heart fills with appreciation and gratitude for Henry and the sweetness he brings.

And then there is Opal, our new rescue. If Henry is love, a bookmark holding the hearth place in the home, baby Opal is joy, all energy, dragging me beyond my old man inertia to run with her in the woods, so that she can run with glee in literal leaps and bounds, disappearing into the brush before reappearing above the brush line in arching leaps, like the leaping of a white tailed deer, an incarnation of freedom having been rescued, running like the first burst of spring with joy at rebirth. Opal running with utter freedom in a field dressed with the blush of spring bloom is one of the most beautiful sights I have witnessed on earth.

But Henry is getting old. I can barely broach the thought of his passing. Sadly, he has many orthopedic issues. His hips can barely raise his body up and when he walks he does so with pain; his gait is slow and limping.

When he was young a squirrel that crossed his path did so with peril. The squirrel would have to flee immediately up the nearest tree with Henry barking at the base. Henry loved this game of chasing squirrels. But now that his legs are tired, a squirrel passes, I see him make an internal calculation and decide, "No, I don't care that much." The squirrel passes with impunity. Until realizing that Opal, the leaping rodent hunter ninja, is not far behind.

Henry is expressing a universal characteristic of age and maturity. The game of life, which was once urgent and compelling, is now looked at with detachment. The squirrel, once a matter of great consequence, is now no big deal. I think I am following the same trajectory. In youth, climbing the ladder of ambition was urgent; there were battles to be fought and won. Now the entire play can be seen with detachment. What was urgent is now amusing, as if the camera lens, once focused in close-up on details of the scene at hand, has panned out to reveal the grandeur of the landscape on which the scene is played. The detail, the squirrel, the battle, is now insignificant, not urgent at all. Rather, life as a whole is seen as a grand spectacle, a spectacle for the ages, a spectacle I embody, for the spectacle is not seen apart from the seer. I, as seer, encompass the panorama and the detail of seeming consequence is inconsequential from the perspective of the camera panned to infinity, to the previously overlooked backdrop, the backdrop of eternity that I increasingly recognize as my identity.

In February during my senior year of college my father passed. I was close to graduation and life lay before me. I absorbed the event as best I could at that particular juncture. Then, several years later, while meditating during a long silent retreat, I started to weep. The impact of my father's death, my grief at his passing, the purity of his love for me, his goodness as a father, and the simple fact that I missed him finally hit with full force.

    We were told by the family who fostered Opal for the month before we adopted her, she was so frightened that she would not leave her crate for the first two weeks they kept her. When we did adopt her in December, early in winter, her body trembled, her muscles twitched in fear when she was approached. We let her emerge from the crate in the living room in her own time and comfort. Months later when spring arrived, when I ran with her in the field, she ran with abandon. She knew she was finally safe and free, winter was over, it was springtime for earth and for her own life. The young leaves on the trees surrounding the field budded in shades of lime, while the maples flowered in red. Waves of wildflowers washed upon the earth in purple. Ferns mingled among the flowers, lit luminous by the sun into shades of bright emerald. A half, morning moon presided in a cloud ornamented sky. Woodpeckers provided percussion, echoing from the distance. Streams rushed downhill through the field with snowmelt. Opal bounded amid tall grasses with the boundless joy of freedom. My neural circuitry could not absorb the immensity of the beauty around me however long I paused to gaze. One night, like the grief at the loss of my father's love which had incubated for years prior to the meditation retreat, the scene in the field returned to mind, the majesty I could not fully absorb in the moment, and then too I wept for beauty.

Spring Leaves

Spring leaves are like kindergarten kids, innocent pastels of lemon and lime, not yet the mature deep greens of summer, lighting the world in bright shades of rebirth, all promise, announcing another chance in the cycle of change to make the world pure, in their image.

2. The God Hypothesis

Perfect Peace

In deep, dreamless sleep I am in a state of perfect peace. Silence and stillness prevail. There is no ripple on the pond, no thought whatsoever. There is no time or space, no boundary, no story, no events, no movement, nothing to tell. I am without definition or limitation, without beginning or end. I am endless. I am nameless. I am timeless. I am boundless. I am entirely alone. There is nothing else, nothing other. I am complete. I want for nothing. Radiant peace reigns. All that can really be said of this state is that I Am. I am, however, unconscious.

The Fall

Then I awaken. Rather than perfect peace, I awaken to definition and limitation. I have ideas about myself and about all kinds of things, ideas about almost everything. I have a name and identify with the name that I was told was mine. I was told that I was born in a particular time and place. I believe that I was born and will die. I have a body and a gender. I have a history, memories, assumptions about myself based on this history, and issues with self esteem. I identify with the nation where I was born. I am an American or an Indian or Chinese. I was raised in a religion, am Jewish or Catholic, Hindu or Buddhist, and subscribe to the beliefs my religion instructed. I have many other beliefs and opinions. Some things are definitely right and some things are definitely wrong. I identify with one side in the political debate. I have a social status and know where I fit in the social and economic hierarchy. I have a financial status and know how things are shaping up regarding money and the future. I am single or married, divorced or widowed. I have relationships with others similarly constituted, along with desires and ambitions regarding those others. Some things I want and pursue - personally, professionally, materially, sexually; other things I avoid. I pursue objects of pleasure and avoid objects of displeasure. I have many thoughts. My mind is busy. I have a lot of work to do. I need a vacation! There is not just a ripple on the pond but many waves. Sometimes I drink, smoke, use drugs or medications to improve my state of mind. I can barely remember a state of perfect and endless peace. I have fallen from the state of grace.

Thoughts

The thoughts make all the difference between the stillness of sleep and the turmoil of waking. Go to the root of the thoughts and you reach the stillness of sleep. But you reach it in the full vigour of search, that is, with perfect awareness. (GVK, P. 411. GVK refers to Guru Vachaka Kovai, see references).

In these three sentences, Ramana Maharshi summarizes the path to peace and spiritual realization. In deep sleep I am in a state of perfect peace and stillness. I am unboundaried being without the slightest trace of unease. But when I awaken something changes, perfect peace is lost and I find myself in turmoil. What changed, what intervened to make the difference between the perfect peace of deep sleep and the turmoil of waking? Thoughts. "Thoughts make all the difference between the stillness of sleep and the turmoil of waking."

When I awaken, mind awakens. (Mind is defined, for our purposes, as the activity of thinking, so "mind" and "the activity of thinking" are the same thing). When I awaken, I awaken into my individual ego-identity, positioned in time, space, and story, with all its situations, ideas, desires, ambitions, problems. I awaken to thoughts about people, places, and things - but mostly people. I awaken to a problematic world comprised of other people in the same boat, and have lost the state of perfect peace. But this does not need to be the case. "Go to the root of the thoughts and you reach the stillness of sleep."

BSB introduced the "tree" metaphor which I will repeat here. The tree metaphor is wide ranging in illustrating how any multiplicity can be traced to a singular source. For now, let's use the tree metaphor to illustrate the mind. The canopy of a tree is complex: many branches and many branches branching off from other branches. But take any point in the complexity, take any branch, walk it back to its source, and you come to the common source for all the branches: the trunk. The trunk is the center, the source, the heart of the tree, the home from which all the prodigal branches wander. Take any branch at any point in the complexity, walk it back to its source, and you come to the same heart and home.

The mind is like the canopy of the tree, comprised of many thoughts about many people, places, and things. But all the thoughts extend from *you*, from the Self, the source from which thoughts originate. "Go to the root of the thoughts and you reach the stillness of sleep." If attention does not wander outwardly but abides at the root of thoughts, you reach the stillness of sleep because *the trunk is pre-branch*, pre-any-thought-about-the-world. In the pre-thought state, the pre-branch place, what remains is the simplicity of "I," mere being, Ever-Presence, consciousness, not conceptualized, just the primal sensibility "I," ecstatic "I," Original Consciousness without modification.

"You reach it in the full vigour of search, that is, with perfect awareness." Perfect peace, the stillness of sleep, absent story, drama, or ego sensibility, is restored *in the waking state* when you abide at the root of thoughts, in the heart, the trunk, the primal sensibility "I." This is the culmination of the spiritual path, abiding pre-ego, in the purity of the source, as the Self, abiding as that source and Self which can also be called God.

The import of "I" is Brahman, God.

Meditation

The mind is nuts. Once you venture out onto branches of thoughts-about-the-world you are in crazyland. Meditation is the practice by which the habit of venturing into crazyland is restrained. In meditation practice, attention is anchored to a fixed point. When attention wanders from the fixed point - back to crazyland again - and this is noticed, attention is returned to the fixed point. Many introductory methods for anchoring the mind were discussed in BSB and these can be incredibly helpful. Here we will discuss only higher forms of meditation.

Meditation can be divided into dualistic and non-dualistic phases. Most meditation instruction is dualistic in that the subject is instructed to focus on an object. Subject-object, inner-outer, me-other, two-ness, dualism. "I" focus on breath or body sensations; music or sounds; outer sights or inner imaginings; positive thoughts, affirmations or mantras. These practices help to anchor and to break the habit of the wandering mind. When the mind returns to crazyland, it is brought back, again and again. Eventually the muscle memory of releasing thoughts becomes firmly established.

In non-dualistic meditation, attention abides at its source. I don't focus on an object, I focus on the subject. I *remain as* the subject, I *remain as* "I." Who is meditating? Forget the object meditated upon, who is the meditating subject, what is the source, from whence does the meditation spring? In dualistic meditation, I anchor attention on a fixed point to prevent wandering. In non-dualistic meditation I am anchored as, I *remain as* the trunk itself, I remain as Self, which is to say, I remain home in pre-thought stillness. This is peace.

In the beginning you practice meditation. Later on you are *meditation.*

Peace

Peace is the nectar that calms the thought-ridden mind. (GVK, P. 456).

Peace is happiness,
beauty of course,
peace is the long awaited joy,
the consummation.

You know that party you have been waiting for, waiting with excitement and then it arrives; the Super Bowl and your team is playing; opening night for the performance, backstage, the curtain about to rise; the recital, the dance, waiting for prom and then prom night arrives?

Peace is your date to the prom.
The door opens… and there she is.

Opal

Peace is the love of dogs.
Some men write odes to women… let me tell you about Opal!

Henry

Henry died today. We brought him to the vet emergency room where he was injected with the potion and his body fell limp. I am grieving. Though he sometimes barked too much and, yes, if we were not vigilant he would run down the driveway to bark at passersby, horses, other dogs - he was a Sheltie, after all - he was sweetness itself, the sweetest disposition, pure innocence looking through his eyes, the beauty of innocence, the beauty of purity, his pure goodness reminding me of something - Love - that I sometimes fail to see in the dealings of men. But as I look up to the sky, do not these wisps of clouds, does not this radiant blue sky and brilliant sun lighting yellowing autumn leaves, does not this speak of the same love shining in Henry's trusting eyes?

I once saw a patient the day he put his dog down. He cried from guilt because, as his dog looked up with those innocent, trusting eyes, the potion was being injected into his veins. I had not yet owned dogs and did not understand his grief. I do today.

A friend texted a quote attributed to Ramana which reads: "The body dies but the spirit that transcends it cannot be touched by death." I am comforted by the image of Henry, freed from a broken, mortal body, broken hips, broken kidneys, released in a doggie heaven, freed from the weight and pain of brokenness, running as joyfully as he did in youth, running and barking, a great smile on his face. I am comforted by the possibility that the potion signaled release, a new beginning, where Henry's spirit of pure joy could burst again to the brim, running and barking, a great smile on his face.

O dear Henry, we love and miss you so. May you be granted every happiness. May we be reunited in a place of light.

Dark and Light

You grieve when your dream dies, you cheer when your team wins, it's alright to be a human being… as long as you know that you are not a human being.

Atman and Brahman

Why is the import of "I" God or Original Consciousness? Let's use the tree metaphor differently, not as a metaphor for mind where errant thoughts wander from the source. With the tree illustrating mind, climbing onto branches of thought represents impurity; consciousness needs to be purified of these outward going tendencies. But the tree metaphor can be used so that the tree represents the totality of things, the totality of the universe, the source *and its expressions*. The branches, in this case, are not impurities but aspects of the totality. The tree represents the life of the manifest universe; each branch and leaf is a meaningful expression of that life. In the first metaphor the branches are not meaningful, the trunk is meaningful. In the second metaphor the branches and leaves are all meaningful expressions from the life of the tree.

Every branch is an expression of the source and embodies the nature of the source. The life in the outermost leaf is absolutely identical with the life of the tree. The life of the tree permeates all its parts. So does the individual soul participate in the nature of the source from which it expresses. Atman, the individual soul, is not individual at all but is the expression and so identical with its source. Atman is of the nature of Brahman, God.

The Four Noble Truths

The doctrine of the Four Noble Truths is the heart of the Buddhist teaching. The Four Noble Truths is a succinct statement of the human condition, the problem it presents, and the solution to the problem. The Four Noble Truths are:

1. Life is fraught with suffering.
2. The cause of suffering is craving.
3. There is an end to suffering: Nirvana.
4. There is a path to the end of suffering: the Noble Eightfold Path.

The First Noble Truth: Life is Fraught with Suffering

The first Noble Truth affirms the reality of the fall. Life is fraught with suffering, which is to say, I have fallen from a state of grace and live in a state of unease. I perceive a world of differences, a world of others. I have opinions - likes and dislikes - about these others, and these others have opinions different from mine. I perceive a world of distinctions. I am confined and defined by a body. I have eaten the fruit of the tree of knowledge of good and evil, mind and ego are born, the impression that I am an entity separate from the totality is born, and innocence is lost.

In the preface, I referred to the existential philosophers whom I read in college. The existentialists are the philosophers of the First Noble Truth. The existentialists recognize that something is less than satisfactory in the human condition, an element of incompleteness or anxiety. From the existential perspective, I am strangely cast away in a strange world, adrift, not knowing where I came from, how I came to be here, or how to navigate these waters. But the existentialists do not progress beyond the First Noble Truth. While recognizing unease in the human condition, they do not fully understand its cause, its potential end in the restoration of perfect peace, and the pathway there; the last three of the Four Noble Truths. The completion of the journey and the directions home are left to the spiritual luminaries.

The Second Noble Truth: The Cause of Suffering is Craving

Peace is the original state. If what comes from outside is rejected what remains is peace... Only that which comes from outside has to be thrown out. (Padamalai, P. 197).

The second Noble Truth states that the cause of suffering is craving. In BSB craving was defined as, "obsessing about your dilemma." People are all walking around preoccupied with thoughts about their place in life, what is lacking in their place in life, their desires and grievances, what needs to be done to improve their place in life. There is always a dilemma on hand that elicits concern.
Let's give craving another but similar definition. Craving is defined here as the "outward-going-mind." "Obsessing about

your dilemma" and the "outward-going-mind" amount to the same thing. Because, while obsessing about dilemma, attention is embedded in thoughts about the world outside. And as Ramana has said, "that which comes from outside has to be thrown out." So involvement in thoughts about the world outside is to be discarded, and attention reoriented not toward the content of thoughts, but to their source. In doing so, there is a setting down of preoccupation with matters of the world outside. Attention is walked back from whatever branch it has climbed onto, back to the trunk. Once there is no involvement in thoughts about the world outside, the peace of stillness presents; resting in the simplicity of pure, radiant being which is as close as close can be, as close as this moment.

The outward-going-mind thinks random thoughts about random things. These thoughts are spoken in your voice - the voice of the ego. The thoughts all pertain to you, your relationships with others and the world in general. These thoughts can be called stories. You tell yourself stories all the time; each thought is another story about another matter of concern. Stillness, the cessation of thought, is the cessation of story-ing. With the cessation of story-ing you abide as being without any story including the root story: I am a body in a world that is other.

So thinking about "what comes from outside" amounts to the outward-going-mind. The outward-going-mind is *worldly*. Worldliness and the outward-going-mind also amount to the same thing. The outward-going-mind is preoccupied with and looks to the world for happiness which, it assumes, will be found in the future through the fulfillment of desire. I am always seeking another moment. The present, what is actually on my plate, is overlooked or regarded as insufficient. I am never entirely at rest in the boundless present, in the original state of peace, because I have an agenda that takes attention away from the boundless present. I am inwardly busy and busyness is the opposite of peace; peace arises in the absence of busyness.

There is no peace while you are chasing an outcome.

Shabbat

In the Jewish tradition, when the Sabbath arrives on Friday evening, all worldly activity halts to make space for the sacred. No use of electricity so no TV, radio, computer, no turning even a light bulb on or off; no flame so no cooking; no driving; no money used in any form or even touched; no work done even to the point of carrying a key in your pocket. Worldliness comes full stop.

The cessation of worldliness is the essential spiritual practice and the thrust of meditation. Because the root of worldliness is the outward-going-mind; thoughts which take up one matter of the world or another. The truest Sabbath is stopping the outward-going-mind; the space that then remains is the sacred.

Be Still

He who does not want to slip from the Self state should not even think these thoughts - "I need this; I suffer because I do not have this," - but should remain calm and collected, experiencing the enjoyments that come from prarabdha (destiny). The reason is, *since thoughts alone are sorrow and bondage*, as soon as thoughts cease, swarupa (one's true nature, the Self) will be clearly and directly perceived. (GVK, P. 168).

This verse from the Ramana canon restates what Buddhism calls the Four Noble Truths and, especially, the Second Noble Truth: the cause of suffering is craving. If you do not want to slip from the state of the Self, the enlightened state, the verse says, you should not entertain thoughts such as, "I need this, I am suffering because I do not have that." Rather, remain calm and collected, surrender to the movement of life and enjoy what does present itself through destiny. The verse goes on to make a powerful statement: Thoughts alone are sorrow and bondage. In other words, suffering is equivalent to the outward going mind which is preoccupied with craving. So as soon as the agitation of mind, craving, and dilemma cease, as soon as thoughts cease, like bringing a camera lens into sharp focus, the radiance of being will be clearly and directly perceived.

"Be still and know that I am God," from Psalm 46 is a further restatement of this idea. As soon as thoughts cease - for what is it that must become still but the movement of mind? - in the stillness that is the cessation of thought you will know God as the ever present truth and heart of your being. Be still (as soon as thoughts cease) and know that I am God (swarupa will be clearly and directly perceived). The entire path is contained in the words, "Be still and know that I am God." The spiritual work, then, is simply the work of becoming still.

Bondage is simply the idea that the present is binding.

Desire

Whenever an expectation comes to fruition in the desired manner, the mind reaches its source (the heart) and experiences only the bliss of the self. On this earth, the same applies when what is desired is attained, when what is disliked is removed... (GVK, P. 196).

Let's say you have long wanted a BMW. You save your money, drive the old clunker to the dealership, make the deal in the showroom, and drive home in your gleaming new BMW. There it is in the driveway! You are filled with joy. Why? Because craving has come to an end.

Peace is your date to the prom.
The door opens... and there she is.

The joy you experience is the joy of the Self revealed, now that the craving that obscures joy has ended. With the fulfillment of the car in the driveway, desire is entirely absent; the Self state. The joy may be wrongly attributed to the BMW because tomorrow, in spite of the BMW, there will be another desire and the initial joy of the car in the driveway will be a distant memory.

One of the fundamental tenets of Buddhism is that all phenomena are impermanent and impermanent phenomena cannot provide lasting happiness. From Ramana's point of view, happiness - peace, the natural state - requires that energy dispersed into thoughts about the impermanent world be redirected. Attention does an about-face, releases its worldly preoccupations, turns within and sinks into its source, becoming still. So the mind that looks for happiness to the world outside is looking in the wrong direction. The outward-going-mind is unsatisfactory for two reasons. First, in looking in the wrong direction, in looking for permanent happiness in transient phenomena, the outward-going-mind's quest for happiness is doomed. Impermanent phenomena cannot quench the thirst of the soul. But the outward-going-mind is busy, agitated, and agitation veils peace.

Recognizing the futility of seeking happiness from the world - it just doesn't work, for all your efforts - you turn within to seek happiness not from temporary, outer fulfillments but from the unfailing source of being; Ever-Presence.

Soup Nazi

In an episode of the TV comedy, Seinfeld, New York crowds line up outside the shop of the master soup maker to purchase a cup of his delicious soup. But the chef is a stern man and if a customer invokes his displeasure the Soup Nazi scolds, "No soup for you!"

"Bhagavan (Ramana) sternly warns: So long as you are seeking something other than yourself as the agent for gaining bliss, there is no bliss for you." (GVK. P. 443).

The Third Noble Truth: Nirvana is the End of Suffering

The desire for objects is the true cause of sorrow, whereas mauna (silence) is the expanse of being wherein there are no objects to desire. (GVK, P. 437).

The third Noble Truth states that perfect peace is possible. Ramana has stated that perfect peace is actually the natural state. Suffering is an anomaly, indicating a misalignment of sorts. A return to grace is possible - call it Nirvana, or God, Self, or the kingdom of heaven. Remember that deep sleep is a kind of perfection. Deep sleep is a state of perfect peace but not because anything has been gained from the world. Deep sleep is nothing but peace precisely because all craving is absent. There is no mind, no thought, no disturbance, no desire; just silence. So the state of grace requires the reversal of the outward-going-mind, turning the mind inward and, as in deep sleep, allowing the mind to merge into the stillness and wholeness of its source. In deep sleep the mind organically merges into its source. For grace to appear in the waking state, the mind must return to its source in the waking state. Then agitation ceases, the simplicity of pure being, perfect peace, the state of grace, innocence, and wonder are restored.

Nirvana is not other than being in its purity, devoid of story-obsessed-mind, which is itself the suffering or bondage that obscures Nirvana.

Mosquito

Some believe that when the kingdom of heaven arrives all will be redeemed. The Rapture, the coming of the Messiah, the Messianic Age. But if the mind remains active the descent of the Messiah in a halo of light will not matter much. There will still be this mosquito buzzing in your ear - your own relentless thoughts, judgments, opinions - that will still drive you crazy. In fact, this earth is a paradise but the mosquito buzzing in your ear makes you crazy in the midst of this paradise. In deep sleep, however, the mind is suspended and perfect peace prevails. That is the kingdom of heaven. Carry that silenced mind into the waking state and the kingdom of heaven is at hand.

In BSB, the phrase used to allude to Nirvana was: "A state, not a circumstance." The Rapture is an inner state of consciousness not an external set of circumstances that will materialize in time. You could be watching a sunset on the beach and, if the mosquito is buzzing in your ear, the sunset experience will be mundane. If the mosquito is silenced, however - and that may happen when faced with overwhelming natural beauty - it's miracle all around, whether watching a sunset or commuting to work; it's miracle all around. So the belief that a Messiah will arrive and everything will be redeemed is questionable. The Messiah arrives when the burden of the individual self is dispersed into the infinite, as in deep sleep, not some external utopia which, if the mosquito is buzzing in your ear, will hardly make a difference.

The Fourth Noble Truth: The Path to the End of Suffering

The Fourth Noble Truth - the Noble Eightfold Path to the end of suffering - can be broken down into three steps: ethical behavior to eliminate chaos from the outer life, meditation to eliminate chaos from the inner life, out of which illumination arises. Peace is the natural state but is obstructed. The path to the end of suffering requires the removal of the chaos that obstructs peace.

If I am a hoarder and my room is piled with layer upon layer of clutter, the space in the room is not affected by the clutter, but noticing the space is difficult. Remove the clutter and the space becomes obvious. Clutter in the inner and outer life must be removed so that the pristine space of Being/Consciousness* also becomes obvious.

Ethical behavior is required to eliminate chaos from the outer life. If I behave badly unpleasant consequences will follow. It's hard to be peaceful while being investigated by the FBI. So don't perform any actions that will cause the FBI to launch an investigation. Buddhism teaches that behavior must be kept within boundaries in five crucial areas: killing, stealing, sex, speech, and intoxicants. Don't cross boundaries in these areas or chaos will ensue.

As the outer world calms, eliminate chaos from the inner life via meditation. Purify the chaos of thought - outward going tendencies - and abide in the pristine space of thought-free, clutter-free consciousness, free of stories: peace.

*Consciousness becomes aware of its own Existence because the two are not separate from each other. (GVK, P. 190).

Being and consciousness are the same thing. To be - to exist - implies being conscious. If there were no consciousness whatsoever that is effectively non-existence. So Being/Consciousness refers to existing by virtue of being conscious.

Space

You go to the Museum of Fine Arts to see the exhibition that has come to town, a retrospective of paintings by the master, advertised for months in all the media. You pay your admission and make your way excitedly to the first gallery. You enter the gallery and, behold, one masterpiece is hung alongside yet another masterpiece! You study each painting carefully: up close, the brushstrokes, the technique; stepping back, the overall effect. You move on to the next gallery where another treasure trove awaits, chronicling a different period in the master's development. Again, in that gallery, you study the paintings. You do not notice the walls on which the paintings are hung.

It is a clear, summer day. Freshly squeezed juice in hand, I step outside to the backyard where I seat myself and then recline horizontally in the chaise lounge. Lying back, I look straight up to observe the progression of clouds across the sky. The creativity of the clouds is amazing, each cloud unique in its pattern, dissolution, and reformulation, each cloud an abstract masterpiece. Some clouds are enormous, thick, billowing, shadowed underneath; others are thin and prolonged, allowing their stories to unfold slowly as they sail across the sky. I observe the richness and complexity of the clouds, the various shapes and shading. I do not particularly notice the sky, the space within which the clouds appear.

I am immersed in my thoughts. Thoughts, like nouns, are all about people, places, and things - but mostly people. Each thought represents some compelling drama in my life, some problem or dilemma; some desire or fantasy; some wound or resentment. I am as immersed in the thoughts as I was in the clouds, the unfolding story of my life as it sails through time. I do not particularly notice the consciousness, the space of awareness within which the thoughts float.

From the oblivion of deep sleep, I slowly stir into dream. In dream the leftovers on the plate of daily experience are digested. The dream ends - space, space - then my eyes open to behold the world. But before my eyes open, not the unconsciousness of deep sleep, not the whirl of the dream, awake but not yet awake, something pristine shines, undefined, indefinable, the eternal backdrop, the wall to the paintings, the sky to the clouds, the space to the thoughts, the space between and behind the thoughts, the space of being, but not being something, just Being. I Am in that space, but I am nothing, without definition, without content, mere blissful being, Eternal Being, within which the pageant of life plays. I Am in that space; radiant, empty, and free.

Cloud Drama

If I look away for a moment, the clouds will have completely reformed in their traipse across the sky. I look briefly away to discover that I missed a crucial scene in the plot! Suddenly the story line is different, how did we get from there to here, I missed the crucial twist and no one will be able to tell me how the plot was transformed. How did we get from an empty sky with the faintest wisp, a minor character, a bit part, and now an epic melodrama is being enacted, many minor characters surrounding a behemoth, the lead character for sure, his soliloquy a half hour in the telling as he traverses my patch of sky, the patch the surrounding trees have framed like a stage upon which the cloud drama unfolds. The behemoth, it appears, has some holes and the holes are whole stories in themselves!

Pilgrims

    The forward wisp of cloud sails like a scout into the blue unknown, like the Mayflower, the Pilgrim cloud, venturing bravely into the open continent of blue space. Close behind, a wave of clouds, more substantial than the first, solitary wisp, more like a fleet of small clouds with dozens of settlers onboard, a Jamestown in the sky. Then come the huddled masses, thick hordes and untold numbers completely overtaking the blue sky in a manifest destiny of sorts, dominating the stage for the moment. But the hordes disperse, their literal moment in the sun passes, and the blue sky reappears, completely unaffected, completely unconcerned, whether there are wisps or no wisps, hordes or no hordes, the sky remains unfazed, unchanged by any movement within it; the blue sky abides in radiant dispassion.
    America in its dense cloud moment thinks itself indomitable. Human civilization in its dense cloud moment thinks itself indomitable. But whatever forms will dissolve,

and every story will have its end. America is one cloud in the sky; human civilization is one cloud in the sky, the existence of our universe is one cloud in the sky, while the eternal abides in radiant dispassion, in perfect support, perfect love, allowing its creations, entertained by its creations, and knowing, "It is good."

The God Hypothesis

The God hypothesis is the proposition that Eternal Being - birthless, deathless Being/Consciousness - is all there is, all there has ever been. The God hypothesis is the proposition that being has not come into being but has always been. While appearances certainly change - like clouds in the sky, like images on a cinema screen - while appearances come into and pass out of being, the being within which the appearances come and go - the sky or cinema screen itself - is birthless, deathless Being/Consciousness.

What has always existed exists now. What exists now is that which has always existed. What has always been is now. What is now is that which has always been.

The God hypothesis proposes that being - the being of this very moment, the being on your plate now (and always), the being that you *are* (for you are not separate or other than being) - has not come into being, has no beginning or end, is always, has always been, is changeless, is eternity itself. This is eternity and has always been eternity. While the changing universe may have a beginning and end, while change is certainly the nature of phenomena, the changeless screen upon which phenomena appear, the context within which phenomena appear, this changeless moment, Now-ness, was never born, will never die, is motionless, solid as a rock. The eternal screen of Being/Consciousness is closer than close, right here, right now, right always. Since the being which has always existed is what exists now, there is no distance to cross, nothing to gain or attain, no distance toward Eternal Being. Eternal Being is perfectly at hand. This moment is the eternity that has never come and will never pass away. But Eternal Being is identical with your being. Eternal Being is looking through your eyes. Eternal Being is what you are. You are Eternal Being. Remember? This is the God hypothesis.

In this world or the next, you will not know any light other than the light of your own being. In this world or the next, you will not know anything other than that which the light of your being illuminates. Therefore the light of your being is the ultimate reality.

3. Verses on Stillness

Radiance

Being is inherently radiant.
Being is inherent radiance,
where thoughts and stories end.

Silence

How to tell the story of that which has no story?
How to tell the story of silence?
What can be said of silence?
Has speech anything to lend to silence?
Does not speech violate the purity of silence?

Intrusive

She was in psychological distress,
and complained of intrusive thoughts.
All thoughts are intrusive thoughts,
all thoughts intrude upon peace.
Intrusive thoughts are bothersome.
All thoughts are bothersome.
She complained of overthinking.
All thinking is overthinking.

Ambition

When playing to this life, I strategize and scheme,
how to meet the need at hand?
how to complete my plan?
my ambition in the dream.

When playing to death,
recognizing my age,
the dearth of years remaining (how foolish to forget),
I reorient toward truth which can actually fulfill.
The pursuit of desire never does,
what the absence of desire will.

Death

Relax. Nothing is life and death… including life and death.
So you die… it's not the end of the world.

Entertainment

    We are all entertained by TV and digital media. But I usually prefer to sit outside in my amphitheater to the sky where I am gloriously entertained by the slow passage of clouds across the stage, their variations of white on blue, while the sun, low on the horizon, illuminates the trees that form this amphitheater in separate variations of glimmer, emerald, and shadow. The sun sets, its reds piercing through the leaves, the nocturnal chorus of crickets begins to play *fortissimo*, as stars emerge from the darkness. This entertainment has been playing for centuries, the hottest ticket in town, before the advent of global ADHD and the need for constant, electronic stimulation.

the faintest sway to these branches,
the gentlest movement to these leaves,
the lightest bounce to these pines,
the blackbird's caw not so subtle,
in the music of this landscape,
the caw departing in the distance,
to leave the native stillness.

Where Thoughts and Stories End

4. Chicken Thoughts

Let's say I volunteer to go onstage during a performance by a hypnotist. The hypnotist puts me into a relaxed state so that I am very receptive. He then makes the suggestion, "When I snap my fingers you will realize that you are a chicken." I am receptive so I accept the thought, "OK, I am a chicken." I buy into the thought that I am a chicken and start to flap my wings and cluck. I am hypnotized. It is very amusing to the audience. Am I a chicken? No, of course not. But I have accepted the thought that I am a chicken and so have made this thought my reality. The chicken thought is true for me because I believe it to be true. Not because the chicken thought is actually true, but only because I take the thought seriously. So a chicken thought is any belief that is real as far as you are concerned, because you take the belief seriously and have made the belief your reality.

The recollection of your identity as Eternal Being - the God hypothesis - is obscured by layers of chicken thoughts, thoughts that are not actually real, but are real as far as you are concerned because you take the thoughts seriously. Layers of chicken thoughts, like layers of clouds, block the inherent radiance of Being/Consciousness, and must be removed through a process of purification. The entire path can be considered nothing other than the purification of mind and body.

Three layers of chicken thoughts will be considered: Metaphysical chicken thoughts, Belief System chicken thoughts, and Personal chicken thoughts.

Metaphysical chicken thoughts represent the domain of philosophy.
Belief System chicken thoughts represent the domain of religion and politics.
Personal chicken thoughts represent the domain of psychology.

Tracing any thought category back to its source yields the same non-dual truth.

5. Metaphysical Chicken Thoughts

The Domain of Philosophy

An ignorant person thinks, through the delusion I-am-the-body, that an individual "I" exists separate from God, the complete and utter fullness. (GVK, P. 244).

1. Chicken Thought Number One: I am a body in a world that is other.

Question:
Is your awareness in your body or is your body in your awareness?
Do you live in the world or does the world live in you?

Answer:
Your body is in your awareness.
The world lives in you.

In a dream you perceive a dream body acting in a dream world. But the dream body and dream world are only a conjuring of imagination and disappear as soon as the dream is released. The dream body and dream world were in your awareness and "made" out of imagination, nothing else. While immersed in the dream you took the dream body and dream world to be real, but they were not actually real. The dream appeared within and was "made" of awareness.

The same holds true now. The waking state, along with the perception of the waking body and waking world, is another sort of dream. So your waking body, just like the dream body, is in awareness. If upon death - like waking up from sleep - this world is released, then the "physical" body and "physical" world will be seen as simply another dream that appeared within the eternal context of Being/Consciousness, which will persist as context for the heaven world to come, like the space which persists through one cloud drama after another. And the heaven world will be another dream that will eventually be released. Because any world - the dream world, the waking world, the heaven world - that comes and goes is like one dream after another, like one cloud in space after another, and not actually real or substantial. What is real is the ever present, unchanging, perfectly close at hand, eternal, Being/Consciousness, the light that animates and imparts reality to all the changing worlds, the context within which the dream, the waking, and the heaven world appear. And that light is closer than close, the light of being that gives reality to this moment, to all moments, without which there would be no moment, nothing whatsoever.

I not a body in a world, I am consciousness within which the body and world appear.

The Standard of Reality

For the jnani (the enlightened sage) all the three states (of conventional experience, namely: deep sleep, dream, and waking) are equally unreal. But the ajnani (the non-enlightened) is unable to comprehend this, because for him the standard of reality is the waking state, whereas for the jnani *the standard of reality is reality itself.* This reality of pure consciousness is eternal by its nature. (GVK, P. 489).

Within the three states of conventional experience (namely: deep sleep, dream, and waking) the waking state, the apparent standard of reality, comes and goes in that it alternates with the other states. And the content within the waking state comes and goes. So the waking state is insubstantial on these two counts. Again, 1) the waking state alternates with the states of deep sleep and dream and, 2) the content within the waking state is always changing. Whereas Eternal Being persists unchanged through the three states, all changes within the three states, and will persist in any heaven world to come.

There is one important difference between the dream state and waking state. The dream state is solipsistic in that the dream is a projection of my individual mind, and all the actors in my dream are conjurings only of my mind. I am not suggesting (though it could be suggested) that the waking state is similarly solipsistic, that only my mind exists and all the other actors that I perceive are my own projections. I am suggesting that all the other actors in the waking state are *projections of the same source*, that is, the same one Being/Consciousness. So we share a common world perhaps because we are each the same dreamer. The dreamer dreaming my world and the dreamer dreaming your world is the same dreamer. Which suggests that you and I, projections of the same Being/Consciousness, are fundamentally one. At bottom, you and I are the same Being/Consciousness - call it God - who is dreaming each one of us, so we are each a projection of the same, one, infinite source, projecting a common world that each of us experiences from a different point of view.

Multiple Personalities

Though I may have a serious psychiatric disorder and multiple personalities, all the multiple personalities - like branches stemming from a single trunk - originate from the same mind. I regret to say that God has a serious psychiatric disorder, many multiple personalities - and we are each one of them. We are each one of God's multiple personalities. But all the multiple personalities of God stem from the same mind and so, at their root, have a common name. The name that each of us uses, which refers to our common source, is "I."

Harm

One implication of this aspect of the God hypothesis is that it is foolish to harm another because the other is the same being as myself. Harming another person - or any creature - is like the right hand harming the left.

Harm is also foolish from a psychological perspective. When I allow the energy of harm to flourish within my mind, I fill myself with the energy of harm, and so stain my mind with bitterness, ugliness, essentially harming myself directly with my own harmful thoughts.

Political diversion: we have elected political leaders who are grossly primitive, who have no cognizance of the metaphysical and psychological necessity for non-harm, for kindness, love, the recognition of our fundamental sameness and thus generosity of spirit, who relish spreading toxicity and ugliness into the collective awareness. Yet the palate of voters is itself so primitive and undiscerning that this behavior, which should be regarded with disgust, is endorsed. At times in history, then, individual ugliness is aggregated into the election of leaders who are embodiments of ugliness.

Success

Popular success - in the short run - is not an endorsement of truth, witness the recent American presidential election in which depravity was elected to power. Sometimes truth and falsehood take time to filter to the popular level. Van Gogh sold almost no paintings during his lifetime. Though he painted transcendentally, he attained no success or recognition. Virtue is its own indicator, not necessarily success in the world.

God promised Abraham that his seed would be multiplied like the sands of the sea, and that very success would indicate God's endorsement. However, it seems that often success - God's apparent endorsement - is showered on art and ideas that are cheap; witness the election, witness many bestselling books and movies. They multiply like the sands of the sea, but that success does not change the fact that the false is false, or that virtue may go unrecognized in the short run. In the long run, however, history will separate the true from the false. Van Gogh got his due; so will the president.

Worldy

Worldly success amounts to fame and recognition, praise and validation by others, applause from the audience, whether self doubt persists or not, whether or not the soul in its nakedness is free.

Spiritual success is authentic liberation, the liberation of the monk in the monastery, whether known by others or not, because liberation may be liberation *from* concern about others, like the solitary liberation of deep sleep, the soul joyously alone in its nakedness, utterly divested of the world, delightedly divested of the burden of the world, dancing the solitary dance of truth, celebrating in the light that is its own light.

Ice Cream

We go to Kimball's, the local ice cream stand, in summer. I will never move from where we live because I would have to give up Kimball's and that is too high a price to pay. The ice cream is delicious, the choice of flavors amazing, and you would not believe the portion size. A banana split can feed a family.

Is the ice cream infinite and eternal? No, the ice cream, though delicious, lasts about ten minutes. Ice cream melts rapidly. If I am counting on ice cream for abiding happiness,

I'm on shaky ground. Ice cream represents the proverbial, "Here today, gone tomorrow."

I go to heaven and encounter a luminous presence of pure and healing love. I commune with this presence before moving on to explore other facets of this realm. Is this the presence of God? No, the presence came into and passed out of experience and so, however magnificent, is a glorified form of ice cream.

All experience is basically ice cream. Experience is always melting. This is why impermanence is among the fundamental tenets of Buddhism, and impermanent experience is unsatisfactory in being unable to provide lasting happiness. The answer to the Great Question cannot be an experience so, if you are waiting for an enlightenment experience, you are looking in the wrong direction. Rather, rest in that which is always true: the imminent space of Ever-Presence.

Some have said, during a near death experience, that they go to heaven and see God. While they may see something magnificent, that magnificence is not God because the infinite and eternal cannot be an object of experience that comes and goes, another form of glorified ice cream. What comes and goes is obviously not infinite and eternal.

The infinite and eternal is the opposite of ice cream. It does not melt, it is always present, it is present now, you can take it to the bank. If there is an infinite, there is nothing other than the infinite because if there were something else, the infinite would have a boundary that could allow for something else. If there is an eternal, there can be no moment when the eternal is not, a boundary that allows for something other than eternity. So the infinite and eternal are perfectly close at hand because there is nothing else.

One chapter in BSB was called, "No Distance to Cross," the fundamental statement of non-dualism. There is no distance to cross to arrive at, because the infinite and eternal is always the case. Unlike ice cream, it does not melt. This very moment was never born, does not move, and does not die. It is now and has always been the infinite and eternal because there is nothing else.

But since there is nothing else, the ice cream at Kimball's is "made" of the infinite and eternal. Remember the 60's song, "Poetry in Motion?" The universe is poetry in motion, the infinite and eternal in motion. Ice cream is an aspect of eternity and, from this perspective, beautiful. Not to diminish the joy of life, Opal's joy at running with delight through unspoiled forest, then finding a stream in which to plunk her belly down to cool off, grinning; the pageant of nature and the seasons, the leaves changing color and falling, the luminous presence of pure and healing love.

Lastly, if the infinite and eternal is all there is, there is no "you" separate from the infinite and eternal. The "I" in its purity is the infinite and eternal looking at its own expressions and knowing, "It is good."

The Matrix

"What appears and disappears is not real." (Ramana to his disciple, Papaji).

I was asked by a colleague to watch the movie, The Matrix. According to the movie, most humans are hypnotized into believing a false reality while the heroes of the movie have ingested the pill that awakens them out of the false reality. But if "what appears and disappears is not real," the standard of reality is not another realm of change; the heroes of the movie are in just another matrix. The standard of reality is the infinite and eternal. Awakening from all matrices requires awakening to that which does not appear and disappear, not to another realm of impermanence and insubstantiality.

Amazon

The fake and deceptive "I", which deems itself to be an independent entity, will perish only when one knows, through enquiry, one's source, the heart. And only when that false "I" perishes will the Self, the true Primal One, surge forth palpably in all its splendor. (GVK, P. 162).

A self declared, born again Christian, wrote a criticism of BSB on Amazon, taking offense to the statement, "At heart you are literally God." In response to the criticism I wrote:

If God is infinite (All) then there can be nothing other than or apart from the infinite. If there were something other than or apart from the infinite, then the infinite would not be infinite at all, but finite, limited, because there is something else, something separate, something other than the infinite: you, me, my dog, Henry.

The belief that you are something other than the infinite is the belief in a separate self, an ego that takes itself to be something that stands apart from the infinite. But this belief - that your existence stands apart from the infinite - is arrogance. The ego believes that it somehow has the power to limit the all pervasiveness of God! And the consequence of this false belief is suffering.

The belief in a separate-ego-that-stands-apart-from the infinite must die. For my Christian friends, this is the meaning of the crucifixion. The ego dies on the crucible of spiritual practice, in the fire of spiritual purification. However, when the ego dies, when the ego capitulates to its source, what emerges is Source, the realization of your true nature as the infinite. This is the meaning of the resurrection. With the death of the ego that suffers, the glorious Self, the God Self emerges. You realize that you are "made" out of the infinite - of course you are, because there is nothing other than the infinite, nothing other than God. God is the heart of your being, what you truly are. This becomes apparent when the ego dies; when the river disperses into the ocean, so the river is no more, only ocean. For my Christian friends, this is what is actually meant by dying and being reborn. And it is a profound, not a simplistic process. If this makes sense, or you want to learn more, you might want to read this book.

Exclusion Zone

There is no place that the infinite is not. There is no "exclusion zone" that excludes the infinite. If there were an "exclusion zone" then the infinite would not be infinite but finite, limited where it is excluded. So if you think that *you* are an "exclusion zone" that is other than the infinite, think again. To recognize this truth become still and in stillness know there is no, and you are not, an "exclusion zone" that is apart from or other than the infinite.

Tragedy

Why is tragedy among the most compelling and enduring of art forms? From ancient Greece (Oedipus), to Shakespeare (Romeo and Juliet), to modernity (Jean de Florette)? I think because tragedy elicits the universal pain of existence, the state of the fall, and the longing for redemption. Tragedy in the theater depicts the pain of the soul weary with the human ordeal. In the Christian story of the crucifixion, however, with the resurrection, tragedy is transformed, the primal cry to the heavens is heard, and tragedy transformed into illumination. This is the spiritual goal: to transform tragedy - the First Noble Truth of Suffering - into illumination - the Third Noble Truth, Nirvana.

The Three Little Pigs

Remember the story of the three little pigs? One pig builds a house of straw, one pig builds a house of sticks, one pig builds a house of bricks. The straw house is easiest to build but is flimsiest and flies with the winds when they blow. The stick house is better. The brick house takes longest to build, requires delaying, but provides the most long term gratification.

I think of lighting fires for our wood stoves. Paper catches easily, flares and burns out quickly. It is used to light the kindling which burns long enough to get the big logs going. The big logs take longer to ignite but provide the most enduring heat.

There is a hierarchy of gratification. Ice cream is delicious but your diet cannot be based on ice cream. It is an occasional treat that flares but burns out quickly. Diet has to be based on foods that substantially fuel the body. Watching a sporting event or a movie is a pleasant diversion but the diet of life must consist of more substantial gratifications than lighthearted entertainment.

So what provides the most gratification? What is the most substantial foundation on which to build your house, the biggest log to get burning which will provide the most long term warmth? Nothing in the realm of change for everything of change is insubstantial. What is most enduring is Ever-Presence, which never fails, which burns, like Moses' bush, forever without being consumed. Let your center of gravity be anchored in the eternal rather than in more ephemeral gratifications.

Ramakrishna told the story of women in India walking through the village square with large clay pots filled with water balanced on their heads. While they might banter with friends in town, catching up on all the news, telling jokes, they never forget that the pot of water is balanced on their heads. While having fun, cognizance of the pot never wavers. You may eat ice cream, watch sports, work, enjoy family and friends, but cognizance of the eternal should never waver. Then the play of life may go on without your being dependent on the play, because ultimate satisfaction is derived from the current of Ever-Presence, beyond the ups and downs of the play itself.

You grieve when your dream dies, you cheer when your team wins, it's alright to be a human being... as long as you know that you are not a human being.

Stimulation

Neglected in childhood, an afterthought to her oblivious parents, she became chronically depressed and distracted herself by engaging in sexual fantasies and excitations, or by binging on sugar and snacks. She had become addicted to stimulation. Stimulation - and all addiction - is the pursuit of momentary sense pleasure that, like lighting a piece of newspaper, burns easily and quickly but will not warm your house. Even if you light one piece of newspaper after another, satisfy one sense desire after another, you will remain cold. What will satisfy, rather than stimulation, is that which can provide sustained warmth; ultimately the inherent radiance of being which burns, like Moses' bush, forever without being consumed.

Which is why: "Bhagavan (Ramana) sternly warns: So long as you are seeking something other than yourself as the agent for gaining bliss, there is no bliss for you." Seeking satisfaction from the outer world is pursuing stimulation in different forms. Granted some pleasures are more substantial than others; a good meal is more satisfying than a candy bar. But even a good meal satisfies only so far. Seeking happiness from the temporal world amounts to stimulation. Happiness must come from that which is truly substantial and satisfying: truth, the eternal.

2. Chicken Thought Number Two: I was born.
This body was born and will die. Whatever was born will die. Whatever appears will disappear. But the Eternal Being within which changing appearances appear, the Eternal Being perfectly at hand in and as this present moment, and which you

fundamentally are, was never born and will never die: the God hypothesis. And by its nature, Eternal Being is spectacularly, jaw-droppingly, incomprehensibly beautiful. The greatest artist can do scarce justice to a single cloud, let alone (as I write) the New England landscape in October, stunning in its multi-colored majesty, nature's most glorious, painterly extravaganza.

3. Chicken Thought Number Three: I am a person.
If I identify with the character that appears within this dream called the waking state, if I take the waking state to be the standard of reality, then I take the character that appears within the dream, the body/mind with its name and history, ideas and opinions, to be me. I am then that limited body/person. If I do not identify with what appears within the dream, but with the Eternal Being who gives rise to the dream, the context of unboundaried eternity within which the dream and apparent person appear, then I am not a mere person, I am the Eternal Being that gives rise to this and to all dreams.

4. Chicken Thought Number Four: The world is physical.
The objects that appear in consciousness are consciousness only. (GVK, P. 184).

Let's say there is a universe. No, let's say this universe is a multi-verse composed of many small universes like our own. Our universe, beginning with the big bang, is just one little universe in this multi-verse containing many such universes each of which began with its own big bang. So we have this incomprehensibly vast Universe containing zillions of universes, let alone, in each universe, billions of galaxies containing billions of stars. And let's say, of this vast universe, that *there is no one in it.*

There is no one in this universe. There are no creatures great or small. So this universe is meaningless because there is no one for whom the universe could have meaning. Who cares? There is no one to care. In the words of the Beatles this universe exists For No One.

But does this universe exist? If there is no one to perceive the universe can this universe be said to exist? Certainly no one cares - there *is* no one - but, in the absence of this universe being perceived by a perceiver can we even say that the universe is there?

Now let's drop a person, a being of some sort into this universe. Lights on! The on-switch is the light of perception, of consciousness. Consciousness is the on-switch. The universe is now perceived, exists for the perceiver, and has significance. So the lights-on switch of consciousness is the switch that turns the universe on. In the absence of the on-switch of consciousness the universe is off.

Does the universe bring this perceiver into being or does the perceiver bring the universe into being?

Your being is the light that turns the universe on. No you, no universe. The light of Being/Consciousness is the on-switch that turns on the vast universe; in the absence of that light, the universe is off. We could call the light of your Being/Consciousness God because it is that which brings the universe into being.

So, if there is a physical universe and *no one in it*, this physical universe, in the absence of consciousness, effectively does not exist. A universe that exists For No One is meaningless - there is no one for whom the universe could have meaning. Rather, Being/Consciousness - Eternal Being - is the fundamental reality that projects - dreams - this seemingly physical universe which is really nothing other than the consciousness of the dreamer.

5. Chicken Thought Number Five: I am not enlightened.
The light of being is always on. The light of being is enlightenment itself. Un-enlightenment is simply the chicken thought, "Something elsewhere will fill my void." If you believe this thought it will be your reality - the definition of a chicken thought. Enlightenment is the removal of the thought, "Something elsewhere will fill my void," the removal of craving. The search for something elsewhere is an obstruction to resting in the light of being that is always on, has always been, and can never not be on. If there is something to attain, it is to withdraw from chicken thoughts - the clutter in the spacious room, the clouds that obstruct the sky - to become still.

*Remove the thought, "This is **not** God."*
*Then this **is** God, it has always been God,*
It is Never Not God,
All God, All the Time.

Outward-Going-Mind = Worldliness = Drama = Story = Samsara

To stay at the trunk, in the pre-branch place, is to not venture into any thought including the thought, "I am searching," for happiness, for truth, for enlightenment, for even that is a story. Be still; without any story. To search is to engage in a story of search, Samsara is the drama of worldliness and desire, yet stillness precludes any trace of the outward-going-mind.

6. Chicken Thought Number Six: *I am an independent person who acts and makes choices by my own free will.*

As an old guy, when I reflect upon my life there seems to be an inevitability to the way it has unfolded. At each juncture it seemed as if I had choice; looking back it all just took its course. Even now as I write I may seem to choose my words. But these ideas have incubated and the thoughts that do come: do I choose my interests? Why am I not writing a cookbook? If I were to write a cookbook, we would all be in serious trouble.

Looking back, the choices were outcomes of "where I stood" at that particular juncture so, while seemingly free, were more likely just happening.

And happening by virtue of what? The power that turns the earth turns all our lives. We are fueled by - not the author of - a power. The ego is helpless, an illusion, while power is the truth that turns us all.

Visitation

I am trying to find a book to read. I start with the Spiritual Book Award winner. Well written but perseverating, get to the point please. What do you want to tell me? Let's move on. I try the National Book Award winner. The style is graceful I suppose - it must be, it won the award - but I don't care about what is being said. Why is this life important? What lessons am I to learn? What is profound in these recollections and musings? Next, I try the Nobel Prize winner. The style is thoughtful, elegiac. But I cannot get past the feeling that I do not care. Now the fault must be mine. These books have won the greatest awards the world has to offer. But the award judges - are their priorities the same as mine? I want to be swept away by truth. I want to see the face of the divine, to assuage the longing in my soul for completion, to receive the visitation of the goddess, to bask in her radiance, to have a spiritual orgasm, the kundalini rising like a tsunami to fill every nerve ending and pore, to moan in ecstasy as I am drowned by the force of life, until that force burgeons and I become mute. I put the books aside. I close my eyes; the force is swelling. I am being summoned. I turn off the lights, the power that turns the earth is overtaking this body and I can only submit. This is what I was seeking in the books and failed to find.

6. Verses on Philosophy

Import

The import of your existence goes beyond the specifics of a given life.
The import of truth goes beyond the existence or non-existence of a given universe.

$X / \infty = 0$

$X / \infty = 0$. X divided by infinity equals zero. Any value - X - when divided by the infinite, in the context of the infinite, amounts to nothing. This is a mathematical expression of spiritual truth.

All values, the content of any experience, the value of an entire universe, or a trillion universes, from the perspective of the limitless infinite, is empty, zero, amounts to nothing.

God is lounging around one day and has an interesting idea: a universe, no, a trillion universes. Hmm and, just for fun, this is what a trillion universes might look like! Nice idea, a mere imagining; a trillion universes is the blink of an eye in the context of infinity.

When the devotee truly understands that the world is an illusory projection of the mind, his mind no longer moves towards it. When this happens, the mind goes back to its source and disappears, leaving the ajata (non-creation, non-causality) experience in which one knows directly that world never existed or was created except in the imagination. (GVK, P. 42).

When you're inside the dream, the dream and its goings-on seem real. You're caught up in the story of the dream. But when you awaken, you realize that you were dreaming, and while the dream seemed real it was mere imagination.

On a practical level, as spiritual practice, focus should remain on the infinite, the unchanging context of Ever-Presence, rather than venturing with the outward-going-mind into the content of the dream. Remain as that which dreams rather than becoming lost in the story of the dream. Remain as space and not cloud, as ∞ and not X.

Incarnations

Some teachings state that the soul undergoes thousands of incarnations as it evolves toward spiritual maturity. From the perspective of eternity, those thousand incarnations are just one wandering thought, one simple moment of forgetting before the lapse of attention is noticed, the fantasy of a soul on a journey of a thousand incarnations is recognized with amusement, and attention brought back home to the infinite, from which perspective nothing has happened at all.

Fullness

From the perspective of the mind absorbed into fullness, whether a universe exists or not is a matter of no consequence. In deep sleep is there a need for a universe? No, there is welcome relief from the existence of a universe. Consciousness' inherent fullness is all that is needed. I Am-ness is all that is needed. I Am-ness is actually all that exists. The existence of the universe is contained within the existence of I Am-ness, icing on the cake, tantra, an opportunity to explore fullness in form, nice but not necessary.

Where Thoughts and Stories End

7. Belief System Chicken Thoughts

The Domain of Religion and Politics

Do not search for truth, only cease to cherish opinions. (Hsin Hsin Ming).

Boxes

He was searching for truth and, when introduced to non-dualism, was cautious about adopting yet another belief system, putting himself in another box. But the teaching of non-dualism is about emerging from *all* boxes and identifications, including identification with the body, mind, and ego, thereby returning to the Unconditioned Mind, prior to its being cluttered with layer upon layer of beliefs.

Beliefs

Metaphysical chicken thoughts are the broadest of the false beliefs taken seriously: "I am a body who was born and will die, this world - the waking state - is physical and fundamentally real, and I - a separate individual - act of my own free will within it." Another layer of chicken thoughts involves belief systems.

Belief systems are fictions if the belief does not conform to reality. I may wholeheartedly subscribe to a religious or political belief, but I may just be a devotee of a fiction. I may believe that the earth is flat or the moon made of green cheese and hold conventions with others of similar persuasion but, if the belief does not conform to reality, I am a wholehearted devotee of a fiction.

On the other hand, I may entertain a hypothesis that I am willing to subject to scrutiny to verify if the hypothesis is correct. If the hypothesis does conform to reality then I do not entertain a mere belief, my belief is true, I am a devotee of truth.

In both the domains of religion and politics, I may hold beliefs that are congenial fictions if the beliefs do not conform to reality. The objective in both domains should be to ascertain whether my beliefs (hypotheses) are true, not simply to rally behind beliefs that amount to a bunch of chicken thoughts.

Religions, as we will see, often contain falsehoods. Since the map of reality is incorrect, by following the religion, I and the world do not arrive at a destination of peace. Similarly in politics, I may hold beliefs about what is good and virtuous but, if my belief is false, the policies I adopt will not yield economic prosperity or global peace. Policies must be in harmony with truth, the way of things, the Tao, to yield benevolent outcomes.

In August, 2017, white supremacists held a rally in Charlottesville, Virginia that resulted in death and injury. In the aftermath of the debacle, on a radio show discussing the event, one of the white supremacists said in a sound bite: "We are here to take America back for white people and to kill Jews."

Such is his belief system. Most normal people recognize that this belief system is not just false but stupid, as moronic as the president who was not sufficiently morally evolved to denounce the sentiment. Yet the white supremacist takes this thought seriously, it forms his belief system, he has made this chicken thought his reality, his *religion*, to the point that he attends rallies passionately advocating for violence.

Somewhere along the line he was hypnotized into believing this nonsense. The thought is vapor, meaningless, possessing as much merit as the thought, "I am a chicken." Yet in both cases, if the thought is taken seriously, by virtue of the fact that the thought is taken seriously, an empty blip of thought vapor can be elevated into a governing belief that spills over into action.

Spirituality is not about adopting a belief system but about discerning truth. Truth is not mere belief, it is recognition of the actual nature of things. The outcome of coming into alignment with the nature of things is a sense of harmony, a restoration of the original state of peace, happiness, love. So there is a difference between a statement of belief and a truth. Truth is true and belief, even if dearly held, even if the belief governs every aspect of your world view, may be false and will not yield liberation because the map you follow is not an accurate representation of reality.

The Downside of Christianity

I am the way and the truth and the life. No one comes to the Father except through me. (John 14:6).

In BSB I referred to the fact that Galileo was imprisoned by the Catholic Church for the heresy that the earth was not the center of the universe. The church took its belief very seriously and went to great lengths to suppress Galileo's position, but the church's belief was entirely wrong. The fact that many people subscribed to the church's belief did not make it any less wrong. In ancient times probably everyone on the planet believed that the earth was flat; everyone on the planet was wrong.

A patient of mine recently expressed his belief system: "Jesus Christ is God's only begotten son, who died on the cross for our sins, and it is only through Jesus that we can gain entrance to the kingdom of heaven." I know many people take this belief seriously but is it true? Like the once held belief in a flat earth, this is a widely held belief that is false. Let's describe an alternative that makes more sense.

In India, one term for the enlightened state is sahaja. Sahaja refers to the pinnacle of enlightenment yet the word just means "natural." So the pinnacle of enlightenment is simply returning to the natural state. Of course this must be so, because any deviation from the natural state results in a feeling of unease, that something is not quite right, out of alignment, a pea under the mattress, a pebble in the shoe. The organism - the soul - wants nothing more than to be in the natural state of perfect peace, grace, where all is absolutely well, where nothing whatsoever is out of sorts.

Early Buddhism describes four stages of enlightenment. One who has attained the fourth and highest stage of enlightenment is called an arhat. An arhat is fully enlightened; using our Indian terminology it could be said that he is in the state of sahaja. The natural state has been restored. This perfect enlightenment is identical to the Buddha's enlightenment. Granted, the guidance provided by the Buddha was necessary for the arhat to arrive at the destination indicated by the Buddha. The Buddha is special because he pointed the way; without his directions we might still be wandering aimlessly without a compass. We owe the Buddha a debt of gratitude, first, for discovering the way and, second, for providing the directions to guide us to the destination. By making use of his directions, we arrive at the destination he discovered; but, once discovered, our enlightenment is the same as his.

A metaphor for this process: the sun is in the sky but is obscured by cloud cover. The cloud cover is very thick and dense so the light and warmth of the sun are not felt. The sun is present, certainly, but the cloud cover must be attenuated to see the sun. Spiritual work requires purification, the attenuation of ignorance. As the cloud cover thins, light and warmth begin to peek through. When the clouds are entirely gone the sun, in all its glory, shines unobstructed. The sun, the light, the warmth were not created afresh, they were always present but obstructions had to be removed: purification, the removal of confusion. The Buddha provides the method; the arhat practices the method until all ignorance is gone and truth shines unimpeded.

Anyone who has attenuated ignorance is transparent to the divine. Because there is no obstruction, because the ego has been completely dissolved, it could be said that God - pure light, pure divinity - shines through this embodiment. This person - if we can even call her a person since there is no personhood - is transparent to the divine.

It is entirely possible that Jesus was transparent to the divine so that God effectively spoke through Jesus. However, in Christianity only Jesus can attain this status since Jesus is God's only begotten son. I would argue, referring back to the God hypothesis, that there is only One Great Divine and all "individuals" are manifestations of the One Great Divine, each "individual" having her source in the One Great Divine. Anyone who dissolves the ego, the false sense of individuality, the cloud cover, will be transparent to her infinite source and will channel the One Great Divine. In Christianity only Jesus can say, "I am one with the Father." In eastern traditions and, I propose, in truth, anyone can potentially make that statement. Actually all things are always one with the Father though this might not be realized. The spiritual work is the process of realizing what has always been true.

The jiva (the individual self), the son of God, forgetting his real nature, suffers, crying and lamenting. If he zealously enquires, "Who is the 'I' who suffers?" and thereby abides in the Heart, he will then realize his glorious nature, his complete identity with his father, who is the Self. (GVK, P. 179).

So Jesus is not God's only begotten son. Everything, everyone - you and I - is God's begetting. Nor does it require Jesus to enter the kingdom of heaven. The kingdom of heaven is perfectly close at hand, the sun behind the clouds, ever present, ever true. In the east, for thousands of years, perhaps the world's greatest spiritual literature has been produced by luminaries who never or barely heard of Jesus. All that is required is that the ego - the cloud cover - dissolves. No mediation is required to access your own source. You are already sourced by that source. Your being is already the light of Being. Simply progress in the spiritual purification, undo the mind/ego, and the radiant source will shine.

So these aspects of Christian dogma are false. The more lucid eastern traditions emphasize the teaching as opposed to the teacher, and provide clear instructions and practices. Christianity, on the other hand, becomes a cult of personality where Jesus is the only access to eternal truth. But if truth is eternal it must be ever present, ever available, without conditions. That is what makes truth true: it has no limitations or conditions. Anything conditional is not truth.

The downside to Christianity is that this falsehood, as all tribal religion, has produced enormous suffering, the very opposite of the Christian intention. There is a progression from this statement of Christian supremacy - no one comes to the Father except through me - to the white supremacist advocating violence at the rally, and his cohorts: Nazis, neo-Nazis, Christian nationalists, Klansmen, cross burners, crusaders, inquisitors

The Abrahamic Traditions

The Western, Abrahamic traditions - Judaism, Christianity, Islam - are rife with false, chicken thoughts. It does not matter that these thoughts have been taken seriously for thousands of years by billions of people. Each tradition claims superiority, that it is more special than the rest. Jewish prayer frequently asserts the exclusive relationship that Israel has with the Supreme. *"Ki Vanu Bacharta Va Otanu Kidashta Me Kol Ha Amim.* Because you chose and sanctified us from among all the nations." While Israel may have been early in recognizing the one-sacred and, as a result, has contributed enormously to world culture for millenia, from the perspective of that one universal consciousness each nation is a branch extending from the same source, each branch with its own unique and sacred character. *All* nations are chosen but in different, exciting ways. Christianity expresses a similar idea that has tortured the earth for centuries: "No one comes to the Father except through me." And Muhammad is the "seal of the prophets," the culmination in the lineage of prophesy. So all of western religion, while true and sublime in parts, is false and fragmenting in others.

Hear O Israel

Hear, O Israel, the Lord our God, the Lord is One. The problem with this seminal verse is that to recognize that "the Lord is One" is to negate the "Hear, O Israel" piece. If God is One then there is no Israel as distinct from India and China; if God is One there are no divisions. Probably more accurate to say, Hear O Peoples of the Earth, God is One, thus We all are One. But let's give credit to Israel for this significant advance in evolutionary understanding.

Historical Interlude

When, in the late nineteenth century, Nietzsche proclaimed that God was dead, he was actually proclaiming the end to classical religion, the dominance of the western church in human affairs, and the incipient rise of secularism. With the loss of the compass of religion, what would fill the vacuum? Religion can be seen as a developmental stage in human evolution, the stage of the last millennium or so, a stage that is being outgrown. The recognition that something about religion doesn't work, the loss of the authority of the church, Nietzsche's "death of God," gives rise to a hundred years of existentialism, with existential doubt only reinforced by the World Wars in the twentieth century. How could there be a God if there is a Holocaust? With the loss of western, historical religion, there seemed to be an absence of truth, hence an age of anxiety. But truth is never absent; it is the very substance of the universe: All Truth all the Time. Truth is closer than close. Simultaneous with Nietzsche's "death of God," eastern teachings were filtering west, as noted by Emerson, Thoreau, and the transcendentalists. Then, in the twentieth century - BOOM - the flourishing of the possibility of global spiritual consciousness in the sixties, the establishment of meditation centers in the seventies, mindfulness becoming part of popular culture, then the more advanced, non-dual teachings becoming widespread in the twenty first century. Dogmatic religion, my-religion-is-better-than-your religion, may have served a purpose in human development, and may have been appropriate in a pre-web, pre-one-world tribalism, where isolated tribes developed solipsistic cultures and belief systems. But truth is actually, universally available and requires no mediation by religion, priests, or churches, because it is the very substance of what you are, of all that is. Truth is perfectly at hand. Its name is I Am. The light that animates all things, the light that makes up all things, the light of being, the light of consciousness, the light of God, is always true because I Am-ness is the most pervasive and self evident of all things.

Trick question. Who came first, you or God? Answer: You came first because without the light of your being, no concepts - including the concept of God - and no appearances - the appearance of a world - could be. Your light *is* the light of God which is why it comes first, the Primal Cause, the prerequisite for everything else.

The End of Religion

Only as long as the mind survives with there be religion. When the mind attains silence, religion will also cease. (GVK. P. 431).

In its advanced stages, like the tapes in the old Mission Impossible TV episodes, all religion should self-destruct. Because the goal of religion is the dispersion of limitation into the unlimited, and the transcendence of all ideas, concepts, and constructs, including the construct of the religion itself.

Steps to the Dance

I had occasion recently to attend a beautiful Bat Mitzvah and a Catholic memorial service. I noticed how, in both services, there were times to make certain movements, to bow, to kneel, to sit, to rise up, to sing verses with traditional melodies, to kiss the Torah, to make the sign of the cross. A lapsed Catholic told me she also had occasion to attend a Catholic Mass and was embarrassed that she had forgotten the movements. Not remembering how to participate properly in her religion, she must be a bad person! The movements are steps to the dance in the theater of religion, inculcated in childhood, which movement to make and when; the child learns the steps and can dance in synch with ceremony.

But knowing the steps to the dance, how to participate in ceremony, has nothing to do with truth which is not something that can be learned. Truth is ever-present and unfailing, not dependent on conditions, whether one goes to synagogue, church or not, whether one knows the steps to the dance or not, as true in this universe with these religions as in another universe with different religions. The Ever-Present need not be learned, only recognize what is always the case; that is truth, to which religion and its ceremonies hope to point.

The Upside of Christianity

The United Nations publishes an annual survey of happiness among the countries of the world. Most of the countries deemed happiest are social democracies. Social democracies are evolved societies and happy because, by willingly pooling resources, much anxiety about the necessities of life is eliminated. There is no worry about housing, education, health care, end of life care. The United States is not deemed a particularly happy country because anxiety is woven into its fabric. There is no guarantee of health care and your life savings can be exhausted if you end up in a nursing home. The United States' culture values certain "freedoms" which, in reality, make life miserable. The right to own any kind of gun, for example, is defended more vigorously than the right to health care, yet this "right" poisons the nation and detracts from its happiness.

If you were asked to imagine a kingdom of heaven on earth, a peaceful, prosperous, and happy earth, it would not be a place where "rugged individualists" hoard wealth while others live at the edge of poverty and homelessness. Rather, Christian love and kindness spilling forth in form - "whatsoever you do to the least of my brothers" - would be a system of governance and human relations that resembles our happiest societies - progressive, social democracies; happiest because evolved societies based on love are most closely aligned with truth.

Family

My children gave me a list of movies to watch and I started with Coco, a charming Pixar animation. One theme in the movie is the importance of family. There comes a climactic moment when, Miguel, a boy, the main character, recognizes that he and Hector are related by marriage several generations back and so are not strangers but family. But where is the demarcation that defines who is and who is not family? Three generations in the movie, but many generations back we come to the common ancestor of all humankind. We are all descended from the same mitochondrial Eve and so are all cousins at some level of remove. When the generations are few we consider ourselves family and leave money to people in our will, sharing our prosperity. When the generations are many we no longer consider ourselves family and feel at liberty to treat people with indifference. But we are all cousins.

On the outer level, the more time and generations pass, the weaker the perceived family connection. On the inner level, however, we are all offspring of the same source, we share a common and imminent source, we are always expressions of the same, eternal Eve. We are children of the same mother. There is no distance from that source, no passage of time, the source at every moment is radiating its manifestations. On the inner level eternal Eve, our divine mother, is universally present, as present now as in the beginning.

Developmental

I was first introduced to developmental psychology when I attended the Harvard Graduate School of Education (HGSE). Lawrence Kohlberg, who developed stages of moral reasoning based on Piaget's stages of cognitive development was still present, toward the end of his career, and a new generation of developmental theoreticians was building on Kohlberg's work. I came to realize that developmental theories had implications beyond those taught at HGSE. Especially when I encountered two other systems: the Michael teachings, a series of teachings supposedly channeled from a beyond-human entity called

Michael, and the writings of David Hawkins. Mind you, these theories are superseded by the non-dualism of Ramana Maharshi, but developmental psychology has its place in making sense of the dream.

The Michael teachings propose that the soul progresses through a series of reincarnations and, as the soul reincarnates, it becomes older, wiser, more experienced and enlightened. Soul ages are categorized as Infant, Baby, Young, Mature, Old, Transcendent, and Avatar. Some of us, then, are new at earth and the reincarnational cycle, just dipping our toe in the water, becoming acquainted with and exploring this realm. Those are the Infant, Baby, and Young souls. Some of us have been around the block more than a few times, are well worn, maybe even getting ready to graduate. Those are the Mature and Old Souls. The Transcendent souls and Avatars are the spiritual masters, well beyond the drama of earth, who come back to teach and remind the earth of truth.

Without relying on a theory of reincarnation, David Hawkins developed a scale of consciousness ranging from zero to one thousand, with a number on the scale quantifying each soul's level of development. At the bottom of the scale, consciousness presents as greedy, negative, and hateful. Toward the middle, consciousness presents as rational and humanistic. The top of the scale is reserved for great spiritual mastery. As the scale ascends, as the cloud cover of ignorance thins to reveal more of the radiant blue sky and sun, more light and beauty shine through. From the perspective of the Michael teachings, those higher on Hawkins' scale are more advanced in the reincarnational process. From a non-dual perspective, the blue sky and sun are always present; advanced souls have simply attenuated the cloud cover of ignorance, removed clutter from the room, so that the space of Ever-Presence can radiate its divine light without obstruction.

These teachings have implications for social governance. Imagine a large family, two parents with ten kids, and the grocery list is determined through a democratic process. The parents get two votes, the kids get ten votes toward the grocery list. Gummy bears and cookies will fill the pantry, with maybe a lonely stalk of broccoli wilting in the crisper.

Since democracy gives each person one vote regardless of standing on the scale of consciousness, wisdom will prevail in social governance only if there is a preponderance of old souls in the voting demographic. If younger souls lower on the scale of consciousness outnumber the older souls, governmental priorities - the grocery list - will be the priorities of the young: guns will take priority over health care, and automobile sales over automobile emission standards. This is all well and good until the survival of the planet is at stake. At some point, the grownups have to be in charge of the schoolroom.

The Wall

As I write this, parts of the American government are shut down because of a standoff between the president and the House of Representatives over building a border wall to separate the United States from Mexico. The president wants a wall to stem the flow of illegal immigration. The president is a very young soul whose childlike mantra is basically, "Me not You, Me not You, Mine not Yours, Mine not Yours." With his wall, he would like to erect a monument to his state of consciousness.

The United States has an even longer border with Canada than with Mexico. Why is no wall required between the US and Canada? Because Canadians have no great interest in coming to the US. Their country is already prosperous and free - and they have universal health care. Whereas many in Mexico and Central America live in poverty and desperation.

Estimates for building a wall, a monument to resentment that Democrats have called "immoral," run as high as seventy billion dollars which does not include the cost of maintenance, and the border patrol expenses the US already incurs. Rather that erect a wall, I suggest sitting down with Mexican leaders, strengthening a neighborly alliance and a spirit of cooperation rather than separation, and deciding how to invest in Mexico to help cure the cause of illegal immigration rather than just mitigate the symptom. I suggest collaboration, perhaps a technological and cultural exchange, or a Mexican Peace Corps, to help develop a first world, robust economy with progressive education, health care, housing, and jobs in Mexico. Once Mexico becomes prosperous and developed no one will flee Mexico to come to the US, just as Canadians do not flee Canada. Central Americans who flee their own poverty and desperation would seek refuge in a first world Mexico. Mexico can return the favor by investing in Central America to create prosperous economies there as well. This is the win-win approach of love rather than the lose-lose approach of hate, at which the president is so proficient.

He has already insulted our closest neighbor and ally, Canada. With his wall, he would create generations of resentment with our other immediate neighbor, Mexico, and around the world. He has taken his "Me not You, Me not You,

Mine not Yours, Mine not Yours," mantra to NATO and has antagonized our most reliable, historical allies.

If the US is going to spend vast sums, why not direct that money toward Mexico's evolution to help create a first world economy? Generations of friendship, a new alliance of gratitude rather than resentment would ensue, and the source of desperation, not the symptom, would be addressed.

By the time this book is published this particular impasse in Washington will be resolved. But the principles persist. Treat others the way you would like to be treated. Let love build, rather than let hate destroy; a primary lesson this schoolroom is here to teach.

If there is rebirth and karma, I imagine the president will be reborn as a poor Mexican who can only stare in desperation at a wall that keeps him from the opportunity to feed his family. Then the lesson - treat others as you would like to be treated, for what goes around comes around - will have been imprinted on his soul.

Evil

Most of you must know what it means to see a hundred corpses lie side by side, or five hundred, or a thousand. To have stuck this out and - excepting cases of human weakness - to have kept our integrity, this is what has made us hard. In our history, this is an unwritten and never-to-be-written page of glory." (Heinrich Himmler, as quoted in Lucy Davidowitz's, "The War Against the Jews. P. 200).

Himmler makes an interesting point: *evil believes it is virtuous*. Evil is so deluded it cannot tell up from down, right from wrong. In Himmler's mind it is a matter of "integrity" to have persisted in murder when faced with a thousand corpses lying side by side, and in maintaining this "integrity" was writing a "page of glory." Indeed.

Where Religion Goes Wrong

When gay marriage was made legal by the Supreme Court, a clerk in Kentucky would not issue marriage licenses to same sex couples, and so defied the Supreme Court ruling. She believed that she was obeying a higher authority, the authority of God rather than man. She refused to compromise her integrity by cooperating with a law that violated her religious beliefs. Conservative politicians sided with the clerk and made much of the issue of government infringement on religious liberty. The clerk was invited by Republicans to attend Barack Obama's 2016 State of the Union address, having become an icon of religious liberty, and she had an audience with Pope Francis. This is now water under the bridge but useful in illustrating some principles.

In Buddhist psychology, seven factors of mind have to come into balance in order for enlightenment to occur. Among these factors are concentration and investigation. It is not enough to be concentrated or focused; concentration has to be balanced with investigation, with keen inquiry and discernment of truth.

Say it's very cold in the Northeast and I want get to sunny Florida. I drive fast, pedal to the metal, barely stopping. But I am driving north so I am going quickly and with great determination in the wrong direction. While my intention may be sincere, my aim is false. Discernment of the proper course - alignment with truth, a correct map, the true direction of warmth, the true resolution to the crisis of poverty and desperation - is essential or I may spend great resources moving determinedly in the wrong direction.

Dedication to a cause can actually be dangerous if the cause is not just. Himmler was very concentrated and determined in carrying out his plan. The terrorists on 9-11 went to great lengths with great dedication - literally giving their lives - for their cause. Dedication must be paired with wisdom or it can further evil as easily as good. The clerk felt that she was dedicated to God by denying gays and lesbians their legal rights. But is she wise? Or is she a baby soul standing up for baby soul values? Concentration when applied to falsehood is not virtue but evil, defined in BSB as *the melding of ignorance with power*. It is one thing to hold baby soul priorities disguised as religion privately, but when these priorities are given power and become public policy we are moving quickly in the wrong direction.

The Bell Curve

The clerk spent several days in jail for refusing to issue marriage licenses to gays and lesbians. She likened her incarceration to the incarceration of Martin Luther King, both moral stands. But there are two gross fallacies in her thinking.

Imagine a bell curve that represents the distribution of consciousness within the human community. At the right, forward edge of the bell curve are the leaders, those most progressed in the development of consciousness, the spiritual masters, the Transcendent souls and Avatars. The spiritual luminaries have always been pointing society toward truth, beginning with ancient commandments and precepts: don't kill, don't steal, don't abuse sex, speech, or intoxicants. Beyond ethical behavior, states the Buddha, here is how to calm the mind and realize Nirvana, non-dual truth. Behind the spiritual masters in the bell curve are the old, wise souls. On the right, forward side of the mean are mature souls, on the backward side of the mean are young souls, with the babies and infants, those least developed in consciousness, trailing off to the left, bringing up the rear in the forward evolutionary march.

As a general rule, more evolved souls will tend to be universalist and progressive, while younger souls will be more provincial, tribal, and conservative.

From the perspective of democracy, the largest numbers with the most voting power will be distributed around the mean, among the young and mature souls who will have the greatest sway in determining what goes on the grocery list of public policy.

Social organization must reflect truth. The necessity not to kill or steal was established long ago. Only more recently has humanity come to understand, say, that slavery is an evil, that all should have equal civil rights or, more recently, that gays and lesbians should be allowed to marry. Marijuana carried mandatory prison sentences; now it is legal with research conducted into its medical benefits (though I also see, in professional practice, its potential for addiction). As humanity comes to understand truth more fully, this understanding is reflected in law and social organization.

The clerk is wrong on two counts; first, in believing that there is equivalence between her moral stand and the moral stand of Martin Luther King.

In King's day, the rule was that African Americans had to sit in the back of the bus. Some more advanced souls objected to this injustice and refused. They understood that the law was immoral, not a reflection of truth but of inequality and hate. The progressed souls who refused to sit in the back of the bus broke the law but were actually mirroring a higher law that society had not yet recognized. At first they incurred the wrath of the norm - the more conservative and undeveloped souls behind them on the curve - but eventually the norm came to realize that the revolutionaries were right. Consciousness progressed and social law was rewritten to reflect the truth that no one should be required to sit in the back of the bus based on skin color, or for any reason.

In the matter of gay and lesbian marriage, society via the Supreme Court has progressed to the point that marriage equality has become law. The clerk, a baby soul, is so far behind the curve that she cannot recognize what the norm has already recognized. So the argument that there is moral equivalence between the visionary's original apprehension of moral truth and the baby soul's inability to recognize morality that even the norm has recognized is ridiculous. The baby soul believes that her regressed morality (actually an immorality that has been discarded by society) is equivalent to the morality of the progressed visionaries. Ken Wilber calls this the pre/trans fallacy, the fallacy that pre-normal values are equivalent to trans-normal values. *Both break the law* but they do so for different reasons. The visionary is *beyond* the norm and the law, the baby soul is *behind* the norm and the law.

The vanguard in the evolutionary march, the seers, represent the forward edge of the bell curve. The seers get into trouble with the masses, the mean at the center, because they are revolutionary. They refuse to sit in the back of the bus. They recognize the immorality of the rule and are arrested for breaking the rule. Eventually the mean will realize that the seer was correct and the seer's vision will become the norm, the new rule. But the left, trailing end of the curve does not recognize the new normal which violates their belief that some *should* sit in the back of the bus. The perversity of their logic is that their moral stand is equivalent to the moral stand of the seer who violated the norm in the first place. In fact, their moral stand is immoral, retrograde, so far behind the curve that the curve has left them in the dust of the forward evolutionary march.

While the Martin Luther Kings move society forward, the very lead in the evolutionary march are the non-dualists, the *spiritual* vanguard who, if conditions are right, end up starting religions. They espouse the deepest truth prior to its being filtered into social structures: the truth of Eternal Being - One Eternal Being is all there is. We are all expressions of, rooted in, and participate in One Eternal Being. This understanding gets filtered into the awakening consciousness of humankind as social change but its origin is in the spiritual realization of the true vanguard, the saints, the enlightened.

The second fallacy in the clerk's thinking is the argument of religious liberty. Religious liberty becomes a bastion for every dumb-assed baby-soul chicken-thought belief-system out there. Every baby soul can claim "it's my religious belief" to discriminate against gays, blacks, Hispanics, Jews, Asians, whomever, and these chicken-thought belief-systems are supposed to be protected under the guise of religious liberty which becomes a refuge for immorality and superstition.

In the wake of the Supreme Court ruling, other cases came before the court with plaintiffs asking to be exempted from cooperating with marriage equality on the grounds of religious belief - the baker who would not bake a cake for a gay couple, for example. So here is a guideline for deciding such cases. Any belief system that is behind the norm should not be considered religion because the belief system is immoral. The court must decide if the belief is behind or beyond the law. Only belief systems that advocate universality and all inclusive love should be considered authentic forms of religion. Any belief behind the norm is unconsciousness masquerading as religion, even if the belief is sincerely held. Remember that sincere belief can be the fuel of evil if the aim of the belief is wrong.

It is now universally accepted that no person should sit in the back of the bus based on skin color, but this reorientation toward truth took a great battle and social evolution. Those who believed otherwise had to uncomfortably adapt their belief systems. Now, who at present is relegated to the back of the bus, the recognition of which will take another uncomfortable adaptation? Animals. Recognizing the immorality in the mass breeding and killing of animals for culinary pleasure will take time to filter widely. Eventually this immorality will be understood and another adaptation made. While the adaptation may be uncomfortable at first, like an alcoholic giving up alcohol, any adaptation to truth is ultimately beneficial. Greater health and peace will be the outcome of this reorientation; ending the mass slaughter of animals for pleasure. Some will roll their eyes on hearing this, but eyes were rolled when African Americans demanded civil rights, or gays insisted on marriage equality.

The spiritual path is about coming into greater alignment with truth through the purification of clutter in mind and body, which brings about the end of suffering, because suffering is a symptom of clutter. At the deepest level, the addiction to the chatter of mind/ego must be released into silence, so that the apparent individual aligns toward and dissolves into his infinite source.

Life

If life is a value then why is life not valued unconditionally? Not just human life but the life of animals, birds, insects, plants. We say that human life is sacred but is life in other forms less sacred? Rather, let life be considered universally sacred, not this or that life, but *life itself.* Let us be more sensitive to all forms of life, treating each with respect, not killing or wounding, even emotionally, embodying kindness, ahimsa, the principle of non-harm. It is time to evolve beyond considering life as privileged in the form of humankind, to life as privileged also in the form of a cow or a mallard, a firefly or a maple.

For practical purposes there will be limitations to this principle for life is eternal and cannot be lost; still sanctity should be the guiding principle to which we make exceptions as needed, first assuming that all of life and nature is sacred.

Methodists

The headline reads: "Conservative Christians just retook the United Methodist Church. The mainline denomination voted on Tuesday to toughen its teachings against homosexuality, same-sex marriage, and LGBTQ clergy."

"It is my sincere religious belief and the formal policy of my religious denomination that gays and lesbians should sit in the back of the bus." This is an example of the opposite of religion: ignorance masquerading as religion.

Superdelegates

(The first paragraphs in this section were written prior to the 2016 election).

The convention has not yet taken place but the primaries are over and Hillary Clinton has won the Democratic nomination for the presidency. Her tally includes superdelegates, the party members who can align themselves with the candidate of their choice. Some object to this mechanism, where insiders not beholden to the popular vote can influence the nomination according to personal preference.

The Republicans do not have a superdelgate mechanism. On the Republican side, an unlikely candidate has won the nomination solely through the popular vote. I have heard it said, "Don't Republicans wish they had superdelgates now," so that party insiders would have more of a say in their choice of a nominee.

In my psychology practice I have been taking an informal tally, asking patients whom they support for president. I truly love all my patients but can objectively say that the more uninformed and uneducated - the least sophisticated - favor the Republican while the more sophisticated souls are mortified that he is even in the conversation.

Interestingly, these less sophisticated souls tend to be covered by Medicare or Medicaid. They are meeting with me, and with their other health care practitioners, through tax payer supported, state provided insurance. Yet they favor conservative candidates and policies that would curtail these very benefits. Unknowingly, they will vote for candidates whose election will cause them harm.

Brexit passed on Thursday. The United Kingdom voted to withdraw from the European Union. All hell is breaking loose this weekend. Essentially the UK may have voted its own demise as Scotland and Northern Ireland may withdraw from the UK so as to remain in the EU.

The County of Cornwall, a poor county (but beautiful! I have many fond memories of camping along the coast) receives $82 million in annual subsidies from the EU. Yet Cornwall voted to leave the EU, essentially voting against its $82 million subsidy. This is like my patients who vote for candidates who would love to curtail "entitlements." Unknowingly, they vote against their own benefits and best interest.

Why would anyone do this? Only because they don't understand the ramifications of their vote. Hence superdelegates. Doesn't the UK wish today that it had superdelegates who could take the popular vote under advisement but still allow for a veto by elders who could steer outcomes toward wisdom, not noise.

If you are having brain surgery, not everyone has an equal say in the conduct of the surgery. No, you want the input of experts, and those experts to perform the surgery. Granted there may be differences among experts, but you don't ask your uncle which procedure he likes best. It is outside of his domain. Yet in democracy, your uncle has as much say as the Ph.D. in political science and that is fine. But superdelegates, some mechanism of oversight, should perhaps have input into the outcomes of pure democracy, because pure democracy has its limitations - and the potential for self destruction, as with Brexit - which can be counteracted by wisdom.

The above was written before 2016. The Democratic party has eliminated superdelegates for the 2020 election. The Bernie Sanders contingent argues that superdelegates put their finger on the scale in favor of Hillary Clinton, and they did. The problem, I believe, is that superdelgates tend to represent the party establishment, the norm. If Republicans had superdelegates in the last election, the eventual nominee, a pre-normal, moral infant would have been quashed. But superdelegates will also tend to quash a trans-normal candidate who represents visionary values to which the norm has not yet awakened. Ideally superdelegates will represent the greatest wisdom, the oldest souls, who are given a say in steering the direction of government.

Progressives

In online reviews of books by various spiritual teachers, I inevitably find a negative review complaining about the progressive political views the spiritual teacher expresses. But what does it say that spiritual teachers are universally progressive? That guidance regarding meditation and enlightenment, the very forward edge of evolution, expresses a world view of commonality, tolerance, generosity, and love? This should give pause to those who object. Perhaps they should examine their conservative views to see if those views are consistent with the spirituality they seek.

Evil Empire

It was none other than Ronald Reagan who drew a hard line between good and evil and declared the Soviet Union an "evil empire," a regressive entity that controlled populations by force and intimidation. If that same hard line were drawn today his own conservative Republican Party, for opposing universal health care, for allowing the climate to implode thus threatening human survival (relaxing emission standards on automobiles and coal fired power plants; absolutely nuts. Today's headline reads: "The worst floods in nearly a century in Kerala have killed hundreds, and thousands of people are still trapped." Similar headlines appear almost every day - fires are raging in California - as one climate record after another is set each season), for suppressing voting fairness among the most vulnerable to steal elections, for gerrymandering to steal elections, for stealing Supreme Court seats to secure power for the minority it represents, for insulting our historical allies while reifying dictators, for backing a president whose guiding principles are *cruelty and dishonesty*, whose guiding principle is not truth but power at the expense of truth, is in the mold of the Soviet Union and on the wrong side of history. Not persons who are always expressions of the Eternal Light and worthy of love but, rather, the chicken thoughts that form their ideology. Remember that even evil thinks itself virtuous.

I see a patient who desperately needs counseling. Her employer changed the Blue Cross policy by which she is covered to include a two thousand dollar annual deductible. She must pay two thousand dollars out of pocket before her coverage kicks in. She has stopped attending sessions or receiving medical care and is in dire straits. Statistically, she has health insurance and will not count among the uninsured. For practical purposes she has only a major medical policy. This is the outcome perpetrated by legislators who, for some inexplicable reason, think it desirable that citizens of the United States should scramble for basic health care. When my daughter, as an undergraduate, spent a year of study abroad at Edinburgh, she immediately had state health coverage and saw doctors with no out of pocket expense.

Constitution

The constitution is obsolete. The founding fathers were the progressives of their day, the forward edge at that time, wresting democracy from monarchy, and the constitution reflects the enlightened consciousness of the eighteenth century but, seriously, that was two hundred fifty years ago! Time for an update to reflect consciousness' continued evolution.

Two of the last three presidents, both Republicans, lost the popular vote. They became president because of the anomaly of the Electoral College, an obsolete idea that allows the minority's choice to win elections.

The president makes nominations to the Supreme Court but the choices of the minority president do not represent the will of most people. The Senate confirms the president's nominees. But the Senate also apportions power unfairly to minority populations. For example, Wyoming, with a population of half a million, has as much representation in the Senate as California, with a population of almost forty million. California, has eleven million *more* people than even the second most populous state, Texas. Yet four of the five least populous states - Wyoming, Alaska, North Dakota, South Dakota - *totaling* only three million, have eight Republican votes in the Senate, which confirms the president's nominees, compared to California's two votes. So, given the way the constitution allocates power, at present, the remote, conservative, younger soul minority holds sway over more mature majorities in the presidency, the Senate and Supreme Court.

As a result, America is out of synch with global evolution, no longer a leader in climate protection or the embrace of multi-cultural diversity. Some factions in Europe now consider America "the great evil," quite a transformation from what was once "the city on a hill."

Untangling this mess will be a formidable political task, beyond my scope. It's time that I withdraw from the fray, from the world and worldliness, turn the news off, and return to meditation where peace may truly be found - in grace, beauty, and the heart.

Whatever events of great consequence may take place, from now on I will not suffer tribulations through them. (The Shining of My Lord, P. 114).

Law

After college, Brian thought about studying law but chose to study science because he wanted to study not man's but God's rules. But law at its purest is a different attempt to discern God's rules and codify those rules into the social order.

Morality

A motivation and outcome of love,
indicates that an action is true,
a motivation and outcome of greed or hatred,
indicates that an action is false;
this is the basis of morality.

Action that are consistent with universal truth,
the Tao of life,
are harmonious and will yield love;
actions that are inconsistent with universal truth,
the Tao of life,
are disharmonious and will yield pain.

Food that is consistent with the requirements of the body,
the body's truth, the Tao of the body,
is healthy and will yield health;

food that is inconsistent with the requirements of the body,
the body's truth, the Tao of the body,
is unhealthy and will yield illness.

Thoughts that are consistent with the requirements of the soul,
the soul's truth, the Tao of the soul,
are healthy and will yield happiness;
thoughts that are inconsistent with the requirements of the soul,
the soul's truth, the Tao of the soul,
are unhealthy and will yield unhappiness.

If a thought yields unhappiness,
the thought is unhealthy and should be rejected,
just as one would reject rotten food.
Love, health, and happiness are compass needles,
pointing toward truth.

The Heart of the Matter

The immigration crisis is actually a crisis of income inequality. Within the US, it has been reported, the richest one percent own more wealth than the bottom ninety percent. Virtually every patient that I see contends with insufficient wealth, while some have more money than they could spend in a million lifetimes. Domestic income inequality is an issue for progressives who want to change the tax structure to balance wealth more fairly. The progressive vision is the spiritual vision which appears revolutionary at first but which will be adopted as the norm in time. The flow of illegal immigration reflects *international* unfairness in the distribution of wealth, with those in poor countries understandably flowing toward rich countries, especially when the rich live next door. Income inequality is a looming challenge for society to solve and, in doing so, consciousness will evolve. (Consciousness is eternal and unchanging and so does not evolve. The evolution of consciousness actually refers to the individual and collective coming into greater alignment with truth, dispersing clouds of confusion, so that the Ever-Present radiance of the eternal can shine more brightly in human affairs).

Another major issue is climate change and the man made degradation of sacred earth.

The Life of Your Dreams

The ordainer controls the fate of souls in accordance with their prarabdha (destiny). (Ramana, responding to his mother's request that he return home).

The assumption behind the "live the life of your dreams" industry is that the world is like Aladdin's lamp, infinitely generous, and all desires will be fulfilled for the asking. From observing the lives of the thousands of people I have spoken to professionally over the years, this assumption is false. Desires not only routinely go unfulfilled but tragedy often strikes - flooding from Hurricane Harvey is taking place in Houston as I write. Did the entire population of southeast Texas fail in their attempts to live the life of their dreams? Did they "manifest" incorrectly? Was their dream for their homes to be lost to flood waters? The universe does not manifest desires at will, and those who propose fairy tales to the contrary are consciously or unconsciously lying. The fact that not all desires manifest is difficult to accept because the soul wants absolute freedom; the universe *should* be infinitely generous and loving. But we have presumptions as to how this generosity should appear.

Consider that adversity is *a form* of generosity; but generous to the soul in paradoxical ways. Adversity requires that we release resistance, make peace with the unpalatable, integrate the unacceptable into our acceptance, include all faces and facets of life within our love. We *become* infinite generosity in our unconditional embrace of the world. The purposes of the soul, then, may best be served when the life of our dreams does not manifest at all.

The hurricane and flooding should be taken for the spiritual message they do bring. Yet another catastrophic storm is a symptom of climate change. These storms will continue until we treat the earth with respect and live our lives in harmony rather than in defiance of nature's requirements.

Failure

Why should one's attempts be always attended with success? Success develops arrogance and the man's spiritual progress is thus arrested. Failure on the other hand is beneficial, inasmuch as it opens the eyes of the man to his limitations and prepares him to surrender himself. Self surrender is synonymous with eternal happiness. (Talks with Ramana Maharshi, P. 319).

Why, Ramana says, do you think that everything you do should succeed? Failure is important for the ego to recognize that it does not control the world; forces greater than the ego and its desires are at play. Failure thus aids in the ego's capitulation.

Failure undermines the ego. But this undermining can be spiritually useful as the ego come to recognize its powerlessness. The universe, the totality is the true actor. The leaf realizes that it has no autonomy, no individual existence; the leaf is lived by, is an expression of the tree and its purposes.

Otherwise the ego remains stuck up like the image carved on a tower, making a pretence by its strained look and posture that it is supporting the tower on its shoulders. The ego cannot exist without the Power but thinks that it acts of its own accord. (Talks with Ramana Maharshi, P. 301).

The earth is in the midst of the Sixth Great Extinction. Species are disappearing at an alarming rate, a rate much faster than the "background rate," the expected rate of species extinction. While the Fifth Extinction which killed the dinosaurs was created by the impact of an asteroid, this Sixth Extinction is created by man, and man may be one of the species to disappear in the wake of his own sin.

Just as the individual ego is crushed by its failures leading to the surrender of arrogance, humanity may be heading toward a cataclysm that will crush the collective ego, and compel a surrender of collective arrogance. But this will also be a great lesson and transformation. We may face a self inflicted death; still, this might be required for the human ego to acquiesce to the organic requirements of life which it now flouts. This planetary cataclysm will result in a spiritual purification as humanity faces the consequences of its arrogance. As with personal failure, this collective failure will result in surrender of the collective ego to the universal will. Humanity will recognize and be elevated to the divine. And, as Ramana says, self surrender is synonymous with eternal happiness.

Charlatans

The "you-can-do-anything-you-set-your-mind-to" gurus. Alright, if you can do anything you set your mind to then try winning an Olympic gold medal. Too much? Try just winning your local 5K. Still too much? Try winning your age group in your local 5K. Even that will be difficult. You cannot accomplish everything you intend. What comes about is what *the universe* intends, which may or may not coincide with individual dreams and desires. Some goals are attainable when consistent with the universal will. Peace comes in having no mind to contend with, and so acting as an extension of the universal will. This has been called, "being in harmony with the Tao."

Fourth of July

It is Fourth of July weekend in our town of Harvard, Massachusetts. The Fourth of July is my favorite holiday for two reasons. First, the fireworks at the Fruitlands Museum, overlooking a great expanse of the Nashoba Valley, held usually the night of the third. This year, just behind the fireworks, the conjunction of Venus and Jupiter could be clearly seen. And then, the morning of the fourth, the Great Harvard Fourth of July Road Race is run, a five mile race that passes my driveway around mile one. Mile five, the last mile, is downhill. Gravity allows me to run with pure abandon as if I were still young.

About five years ago I started to feel sciatic twinges in my right leg. I did what stretches I could to alleviate the discomfort but did not pay the twinges much mind. During the last year, however, the discomfort has become pronounced and chronic and I have to think twice about running at all. I have shifted to cycling as my primary form of exercise because cycling does not trigger the sciatic pain. The symptom which was once mildly annoying is now altering my way of life.

We live in the Northeast rainforest where fireflies emerge around the fourth. Sure enough, there is some terrestrial twinkling out among the dark woods. But there is no cricket song. The woods have gone silent. We have lived here for twenty five years and never have the woods been silent. I have always loved sitting outside after dark, meditating to what I have called "the earthbound Om, the music of the earthly sphere." This year there is no earthly music, just silence.

As I was making my way toward the road after the fireworks, out of the Fruitlands Museum grounds, I walked past a long line of cars idling one after another, each waiting to break out of the parking bottleneck. I breathed the exhaust of one car after another. It was clear that each car exhaust was spilling toxicity into the air, into my lungs, and that this soiling of the pristine night air was sin. Who wants to breathe poison; why do we then as a society consider it acceptable to poison the air en masse?

When the internal combustion engine was invented little thought was given to the poisons it would emit into sacred space. Now we take poisoning the air for granted as if it were inconsequential.

But it is not inconsequential. We live in a forest and there is no cricket song. Perhaps an entomologist can offer an explanation; I fear this is a first symptom of a poisoned earth, a symptom that may seem like a small annoyance at first before it grows more pronounced and painful and entirely alters our way of life.

We are in the midst of the Sixth Great Extinction. The Fifth Great Extinction was the extinction of the dinosaurs, caused by an asteroid colliding with the earth. This Sixth Extinction is not the result of a cosmic collision but of man's behavior, man's sin.

What is sin? Sin is deviation from the natural order and, because it is disharmonious its consequence is suffering. Spilling toxicity into the air is sin. The first suffering consequent on man's sin is the disappearance of crickets. The last suffering consequent on man's sin may be the disappearance of man. The earth will then have millions of years to re-diversify once the cause of the extinction has been eliminated.

BMW

Suddenly the gorgeous 2013 BMW 1 Series that I bought for my daughter and which I will soon inherit when my daughter moves to the city and no longer needs a car, 2013, the last year the 1 Series was made, small, sporty, two door coupe, nimble, turns on a dime, classic, understated styling, black on black, Premium Package, Cold Weather Package, Navigation, iDrive, Harman Kardon, suddenly this gorgeous machine feels vaguely dirty, obsolete, partaking of the ancient technology, requiring fossil fuels that have incubated in the earth for billions of years and which we will exhaust into the air in one century, spewing poisons. I would rather this gorgeous machine were equipped with solar collectors on its roof, ran clean, and for the cost of a little range, I could hear the din of crickets at night while the solar, battery-powered engine ran silently.

Good news. The cricket chorus sang in full voice later that summer.

8. Personal Chicken Thoughts

The Domain of Psychology

The broadest layer of chicken thoughts is the metaphysical layer, the domain of philosophy. This is the foundation for the other layers of thoughts which define the person. The foundational, metaphysical thoughts are the basic assumptions upon which the rest of the ego-edifice is built: "I" take myself to be a body who lives in a physical, substantially real world.

Truer to say the world is a dream of consciousness and not physical, is not external and other but an expression of that very consciousness, and the body is one form within that expression, like a dream body is in a dream. But the dreamer is beyond the dream; the Ever-Present Self is beyond, and abides, through all the transient particulars of the dream.

Assume for a moment that there is life after death. In that case, once the body dies, there will be an "I" who will persist independent of the physical body. This apparently physical world will then be seen as something momentary, not substantial at all, that will have given way to a "more real" world. The next "heaven" world will be seen as substantial. But the heaven world too will, at some point, be released and seen as yet another insubstantial realm. What is actually substantial is the context (like the sky) within which all worlds (like one cloud after another) appear and which abides through all the changes of worlds, and changes within each world. That is the imminent Self, perfectly close at hand, unfailing and Ever-Present, because it is the very source from which the dream emerges.

As you approach what is most intimate, you approach the eternal.

Upon this foundational, metaphysical layer of chicken thoughts I adopt a series of belief system chicken thoughts that form my world view. These belief systems represent the domain of religion and politics, my leanings, how I orient myself toward and give meaning to the dream. I may identify with a religion or political philosophy. But these belief systems only have merit if they conform to truth, to the actual lay of the land. If I hold beliefs that are not true, that do not conform to reality, if my map of meaning is inaccurate, then my individual world and the collective world in which I live, a world that has similarly adopted a series of erroneous beliefs, will be unhappy because misaligned. I and the world will not be correctly aligned to reality because we hold to an inaccurate map. Adopting a belief system that does not conform to truth will even yield evil if the falsehood is profound yet controls the reins of power.

It could be said that refining the map by learning from evolutionary mistakes, individual and collective, is the purpose of this world; to come into greater and eventually complete alignment with reality, yielding bliss. Pain is a symptom of misalignment; bliss is the natural condition that arises when misalignment is healed. Bliss is a compass needle pointing toward truth.

Chicken thoughts - false beliefs taken seriously, often as a result of early childhood conditioning - define the ego. But truth is undefined and unlimited. So a process of spiritual purification is required to rid the mind of its false identifications, like clearing clutter from a room, leaving only pristine, radiant space. This is where meditation and spiritual practice come in: uncluttering, unconditioning the mind of its distorting filters.

It is easy to see in hindsight the social inaccuracies that previous historical eras made. Was a brutal Civil War really necessary to discern the immorality of slavery? Apparently. It is more difficult to recognize the distortions at play at present, which form the battleground for current political debate. As a general rule, as with the Civil War, progressive policies are evolutionary and forward seeing, while conservative policies represent less developed views that resist change. This is, again, easily seen with historical perspective where battles were fought to institute change that is now taken for granted, the morality of which seems obvious, but which required the awakening vision to overcome resistance (women's rights, civil rights, gay rights, climate change). At present, in America, political battles are fought over guns, health care, and immigration, and I read this morning that enormous crowds in England are protesting Brexit, a conservative electoral victory that is actually an evolutionary step backwards. Conservatism holds much power in the US as well but its policies - border walls, for example – are regressive.

Politics and lawmaking should be an attempt to govern society based on spiritual truth, to bring man's law into harmony with spiritual law, the Tao, the true nature of things, thus legislating love into law by acknowledging our fundamental sameness, treating others as we would like to be treated.

Religion, similarly, is only useful to the extent that its beliefs conform to truth. Religions tend to claim exclusive ownership to truth thereby fragmenting believers from those with different beliefs. If God is One, any religious belief that creates factions and divisions must be false.

In building the ego edifice, metaphysical ideas about the reality and substantive nature of the world, and belief systems that make meaning within that world are assumed. With personal chicken thoughts, the egoic, personal identity is formed.

I may write a complete book on mental health, how mental health is achieved; the domain of psychology. Ultimately, mental health is synonymous with spiritual realization, alignment with truth. For now, let's cover some basic principles, how the ego is a veering away from heart via mind, thus generating unhealth and unhappiness. What follows are the basic rules of mental health.

Don't Make Yourself Sick

The First Rule of Mental Health is: *Don't Make Yourself Sick*.
If you make yourself sick, then you will be sick.
If you don't want to be sick, don't make yourself sick.

Because,

If you make yourself sick, then you will be sick.
If you don't want to be sick, don't make yourself sick.

Every day I speak with people who are adept at making themselves sick, who need to recognize how they make themselves sick, and to cut out making themselves sick. If you are making yourself sick, cut it out - or you will be sick.

Attention Amplifies

How do you make yourself sick?
The Second Rule of Mental Health is: *Attention Amplifies*.
What you pay attention to, you amplify in your experience. To what do you pay attention? Do you pay attention to grace or to dilemma?

Every Thought Has a Taste

The Third Rule of Mental Health is: *Every Thought has a Taste*.
Some thoughts have a good taste, some thoughts have a bad taste.

Food that is consistent with the requirements of the body,
the body's truth, the Tao of the body,
is healthy and will yield health;
food that is inconsistent with the requirements of the body,
the body's truth, the Tao of the body,
is unhealthy and will yield illness.

Thoughts that are consistent with the requirements of the soul,
the soul's truth, the Tao of the soul,
are healthy and will yield happiness;
thoughts that are inconsistent with the requirements of the soul,
the soul's truth, the Tao of the soul,
are unhealthy and will yield unhappiness.

If a thought yields unhappiness,
the thought is unhealthy and should be rejected,
just as one would reject rotten food.
Love, health, and happiness are compass needles,
pointing toward truth.

    Thoughts of peace, love, beauty, forgiveness, kindness, acceptance, generosity, have a good taste. The good taste tells you that the thought agrees with, is in harmony with the Tao of the organism, is wholesome, healthy, uplifting. Amplifying thoughts with a good taste by giving those thoughts attention will give the psyche the good taste of those thoughts.

    Thoughts of hatred, anger, resentment, failure, fear, worry, have a bad taste. The bad taste tells you that the thought does not agree with, in not in harmony with the Tao of the organism, is unwholesome and unhealthy. Amplifying thoughts with a bad taste by giving those thoughts attention will give the psyche the bad taste of those thoughts. Amplifying bitter, bad tasting thoughts is how you make yourself sick.

    If you ate a fruit and realized that the fruit was rotten, you would immediately spit out, you would not continue to eat the fruit. In the domain of thought, out of habit and nonawareness, rotten thoughts are consumed one after the other, thus making the organism sick.

BSB described a path with three stages: Negative-thinking, Positive-thinking, and No-thinking. Negative thinking is how you make yourself sick: amplifying bad-tasting, sick-making thoughts. Using our metaphor of the tree, Negative-thinking is the process of climbing out onto branches of thought, farther from the heart, by telling yourself all kinds of outward-going stories about the world and yourself. This is craziness. Positive-thinking is the domain of spiritual practice, restraining the outward-going mind and its negative tendencies and directing attention back toward the heart by consciously amplifying healthy thoughts, using the mind to good effect. Abiding in the heart, the place of peace and inherent radiance, is the stage of No-thinking.

Cutting out Negative-thinking is a "Thou Shalt Not" process. Refrain from toxic behavior in outer conduct, certainly, but also in inner, cognitive, thought behavior. In BSB this process was labeled "defense."

Amplifying Positive-thinking by holding to healthy thoughts is a "Thou Shalt" process. Deliberately amplify joy by holding to healthy conduct and healthy thoughts, breaking the habit of repetitive, negative thinking. In BSB this process was labeled "offense."

Once you have already engaged in Negative-thinking, climbed into the canopy of the tree, out onto branches of thought - back to crazyland - by amplifying toxic thinking, the process of reversing course and heading back to the trunk, the heart, may be done by means of Positive-thinking. Positive-thinking is a healthy use of mind. Positive-thinking has the effect of saying, "Hold on. Stop going outward, in the wrong direction. Change course, head back home." I may do this by consciously holding to a healthy thought like peace or kindness. Or I may hold to more elaborate affirmations that engage the mind more significantly. By consciously holding to positive thoughts I deliberately use attention to amplify health, to move closer to the inherent radiance of the heart, resisting the bad habit of climbing farther from the heart, out into ego-land, out into crazy-land, thus making myself sick.

The more advanced stage of No-thinking (which is what this book is really about) goes beyond the mind to abiding in the inherent stillness and radiance of the heart. The name of the heart is "I," the pure light of being. However, when the light of "I-ness" is projected outward through a negative lens, and negative thought/stories are amplified, you make yourself sick.

Negative thought/stories - I am not good enough, I have no future, I am angry, I resent that racial group for ruining my country, I want that person or thing very badly - are chicken thoughts, have no reality, are fictions, but may seem entirely real if taken seriously. The Self has no story, is pure being, pure I-ness, the trunk of the tree before climbing onto any branch.

Losing focus allows negativity to amplify. The more lost you get in the process of Negative-thinking the greater the loss of mental health. Positive-thinking applies conscious control to thoughts, the restoration of focused attention. Becoming well requires releasing, first, thoughts that make you sick and, second, all thoughts so as to abide in stillness.

The two primary psychological maladies are depression and anxiety. Depression is generated when I amplify thoughts of failure or hopelessness. Anxiety is generated when I amplify thoughts of fear or worry. These thoughts all have a bitter taste. Yet every day I speak to people who, with considerable determination, dwell on failure or hopelessness, fear or worry, amplifying toxicity in their psyche, thus making themselves sick.

The Mind is the Residue of the Past

The Fourth Rule of Mental Health is: *The Mind is the Residue of the Past.*

Now that winter is over, the windows are covered with muck. Time for spring cleaning! The glass is not fundamentally affected by the muck and, once cleaned, the glass' pristine state will be restored. Light will shine through without obstruction. But the muck, the residue of months' assault by weather, needs to be removed. The glass needs to be purified of the residue of the past.

The mind and its thoughts pertain to the past. The mind's stories pertain to what is already known, what is uniquely of concern given where you stand. The conversation in your head is uniquely your conversation, given past life experience, what remains from the past, what forms the contents of your inbox. The mind is encumbered with these contents. Preoccupation with matters from the past prevents the mind from resting in the radiant space of Ever-Presence. Granted, stories about the future can be devised but those stories are variations on the already known.

The residue of the past also refers to conditioning, how the mind has been programmed, imprinted, brainwashed, hypnotized by past experience to create patterns of self and world regard; the habits of mind, the template through which the world is filtered. These habits need to be recognized and bad habits broken. Then the world is seen afresh, not filtered through a lens that is the residue of past experience.

Anchor

The Fifth Rule of Mental Health is: *Anchor* (or *Hold)*.

The outward-going-mind strays into thoughts regarding the past, the open windows on the desktop of thought, the news and matters of the day. Spiritual practice amounts to anchoring this unbridled, outward-going movement.

Thousands of meditation techniques and guided meditations can be found online. If the mechanics of mind are well understood, all the techniques can be placed into a few categories. But the foundation for all the techniques is the principle of anchoring or holding. The outward going tendency of unbridled thought must be anchored, by holding attention either to positive, healthy thoughts or images, or by holding attention to non-cognitive phenomena like body sensations - including the body sensation of breathing - or to visual or auditory stimuli. In any case, the outward-going-mind's tendency to dwell on the residue of the past is restrained through anchoring or holding. Non-dual meditation - Ramana's self-inquiry - requires that attention holds to the I-thought, the common denominator in all experience. The anchor then is not an object of perception but the subject. Eventually attention sinks into the source of subjectivity: consciousness or being in its purity.

The path can be summed up as "hold to the heart," where *holding* is key. The mind has the bad habit of wandering like an untrained puppy into all kinds of mischief. This amounts to wandering into the world, into worldliness, the mind's involvement in everything outer. Holding requires that mind hold to and become absorbed in the heart, resist the pull into thought and world, and abide in the non-world, the endless, pure being, the sacred.

Mental Health Summary

Your mind is a power tool. As with any power tool, you have to operate it correctly or you can hurt yourself. You have to make sure you are operating your mind well.

Attention amplifies. Whatever you give attention to you will amplify in your experience.

Every thought has a taste. Some thoughts, like thoughts of peace and fulfillment, taste good. Other thoughts, like fear or panic, taste bad. If you ate something that tasted bad, that was rotten, you would spit it out. If you kept eating the rotten food you'd get sick. The bad taste tells you that the food is unwholesome. Same with thoughts. If the thought has a bad taste, you should spit it out, try not to amplify it, or you can get sick. This is an improper use of mind, amplifying bad tasting thoughts.

If you dwell on thoughts of catastrophe, having a panic attack on a plane, for example, you are effectively meditating on catastrophe and amplifying the feeling of catastrophe. But if you can amplify catastrophe you should also be able to amplify peace, right? Meditations are exercises in keeping attention anchored to thoughts of peace and rejecting the mind's wandering into thoughts that taste of fear. If you can anchor your attention in thoughts of peace, or the breath, whatever works as an anchor, and refuse to dwell on fear, you will amplify peace in your experience, this is a good use of mind.

So anchoring the mind against its bad habit of wandering into harmful thoughts is an important skill. Build the concentration muscle, the ability to anchor or hold, the ability to keep attention where you want it, resisting the mind's tendency to wander, like an untrained puppy, into mischief.

9. Verses on Psychology

Radiance Revisited

Being is inherently radiant.
Being is inherent radiance,
if you do not make yourself sick,
by amplifying mind/ego.

Moral Error

He committed a sin of sorts by having an affair. He recognizes that he committed a painful moral error which, upon reflection, he is not likely to repeat. But he cannot stop heaping on self abuse out of guilt for his behavior. In doing so, is he not committing yet another moral error? If further lessons are to be learned from the original error, reflection may serve some purpose. But once the lessons have been learned reflection turns into rumination, and becomes today's moral error that actually stands the possibility of correction.

Reverse the Golden Rule

For those who "beat themselves up" the golden rule should be reversed, that is, treat yourself at least as well as you would treat others.

Be the Source of Your Own Radiance

As a teen he felt insecure with the girls, feared and anticipated their rejection which he took very personally. Now in mid-life and married, the residue of insecurity remains. While he depends on his wife to radiate love towards him, when her love is withdrawn, when they argue or her glance of interest falls elsewhere, his insecurities are triggered, he becomes angry and agitated. He has not recognized that he *is* radiance, made out of radiance, and can be the source of his own radiance.

If you depend on love to come from outside, you're on shaky ground because the radiance of that love can always be withdrawn; outer radiance is conditional. However, the inner sun of being, the radiance of I Am-ness is unconditional, always present and shining. When cognizant of the unfailing radiance of Self, outer radiance - fortune smiling favorably - becomes icing on the cake, nice but not necessary. Be the source of your own radiance, which is never absent and can never be lost. Comfortably seated in the heart, let fortune smile favorably or not, as it will. It won't matter that much one way or the other.

Freedom

Though married, she wanted the freedom to pursue every sexual interest that struck her fancy; she resented her marital commitment which felt like bondage. I think she had it backwards. Desire is bondage; freedom is freedom from desire. We are bound by what we desire; only when the mind is free of the restlessness of its urges can there be peace.

You Can't

The one girl in a brood of boys, her old world father kept her on a tight leash and under strict supervision, allowed her little access outside the home so as to prevent anything untoward, protected her honor while quashing her spirit. The inevitable message was, "You can't. You can't go out with friends, you can't be free, something bad might happen." Later in life she developed an autoimmune disease, her body effectively saying, "You can't. You can't make plans with friends for the weekend, your body might not cooperate. You can't pursue your ambitions, your body might not allow."

I wonder whether her body learned the lesson well, the hypnosis "You can't" internalized even in her cells so that, to be free, her spirit would have to wrest freedom from the conditioned mire of dejection.

Addicted to No

Profoundly depressed, refusing all good faith efforts at help, he was addicted to "No." This is unfortunate because, by virtue of the light of being always being switched on, the universe is perpetually proclaiming, "Yes."

Gardening

He was beaten up emotionally by his mother, then by his bosses, and became chronically depressed. He dreamed of owning a house where he could garden his own land. But he would need first to garden his soul, bringing his soul to blossom, so that the outer circumstances of life could flourish in turn, bringing his dream to fruition.

The Challenge Place

She had a stroke at the age of fourteen. She was an early adolescent dealing with the usual turbulence of that age but suddenly perception itself went garbled. She was rushed to Massachusetts General Hospital where she spent her fifteenth birthday. Tragically, the stroke disabled the right side of her body. Though now, at nineteen, she can drive a modified car with her left leg, while driving she cannot raise her right arm to change the station on the radio. I ask about her mood on a scale of zero to ten, zero being entirely depressed. When she was fifteen, she says, body disabled, no longer able to attend school, no friends, requiring a tutor to come to her home, she was minus two hundred. For a long time she wanted to die and death remains a background consideration. "It just makes no sense. What sense is there to a world where a child of fourteen is disabled by a stroke?"

In heaven everything is a piece of cake. In heaven there is no illness, no strokes, no pollution, no poverty, no frustration. In heaven this clunky physical body with all its vulnerabilities, its mundane aches and pains and catastrophic failures is absent.

But this place was designed with a different purpose in mind. This is the challenge place.

We come here expecting a heaven, expecting all our desires and dreams to be fulfilled. We do not expect to encounter disappointment or failure. We do not expect to be challenged to our depths and so have our weaknesses revealed. But that is the purpose of this place. For in confronting weakness and rising to the challenge we grow, we become strong, wise, more attuned to spiritual reality, divested of ego. We come precisely to have the delusion of ego unveiled. This is, therefore, an incredibly useful place for spiritual development. In surrendering the suffering of ego we transform into the divine harmony, and the challenges of this place further that objective. This is the challenge place. Once ego is surrendered then, magically, this place assumes the face of heaven. Revelation! When we are able to turn this realm into a heaven, when we overcome the personal and collective weakness this place reveals, it becomes the heaven we sought, and so will have served well its purpose of transformation.

Grandeur

That which is worth taking up is the self enquiry that reveals jnana (knowledge); that which is worth enjoying is the grandeur of the Self; that which is worth renouncing is the ego-mind; that in which it is worth taking refuge, to eliminate sorrow completely, is one's own source, the Heart. (GVK, P. 237).

When you fall in love, powerfully in love, say you're in love and this god/goddess is *way* too good for you, too good because their beauty, their grandeur inspires awe. As a meditation, hold to the grandeur you see in this beautiful other. Amplify your appreciation, savor, commune with the magnificence this beautiful being manifests.

So what might this god/goddess see in you? They see *your* grandeur. As a meditation, recognize your grandeur. They see *something*, right, they see *you* as a manifestation of divine beauty. So be in touch with, hold to the beauty this beautiful being sees in you, your own divinity, discover or remember your own majesty, your own grandeur, the grandeur of the Self that is your heart, simply spectacular.

Integrity

Rick wants to open a used car lot. He goes to the auto auction to purchase cars for his lot but is not allowed to drive the cars prior to purchase. He must make judgments on looks alone. He purchased one car that looked good but vibrated soon after it hit the road. He purchased another car that looked good but later realized that the car was full of rust. The rust had been impeccably covered with tape and a paint job. The paint was flawless, the car looked beautiful but the beauty was all on the surface. The car lacked structural integrity.

Josie was swept away by David. During their courtship, he hired a limo to spirit her away to the city; she felt like a princess. That was a new and thrilling experience because she never felt as if her alcoholic mother loved her. She moved into his gleaming new house with the granite counter tops and artisan tiled bathrooms. But after moving in she realized he was also an alcoholic, a mean drunk and a narcissist at that. She was there only to satisfy his needs. His promises were all on the surface. How, she asked, would she be able to trust her judgments in the future? The person you choose must have integrity, I said. That is perhaps the most important quality. The surface may gleam but only if the underlying structure is sound, will the promise he offers be fulfilled.

Marriage

I rarely see couples in marital therapy. Usually couples enter the room with rage flying, they come as a last resort, and the rage flies early and often. I agreed to see a couple recently and, in the first session, Tom said, "We don't usually get this far into the conversation." In other words, without the referee, the rage prevents the discussion of grievances from progressing. With the referee allowing each person their say, the discussion can progress farther into the thorny areas. I sometimes think I should wear a black and white striped jersey and carry penalty flags in my pockets that I throw when the rules of civil discourse are broken. Flag thrown; interrupting, ten yard penalty, loss of down.

Tova is seriously pursuing her spiritual path and recently attended a silent meditation retreat. She has longstanding conflicts with her husband. She thinks, if she can develop spiritually, if she can become less reactive, if she learns to refrain from her part in setting the rage flying, her marriage will improve.

The intersection with the spiritual is best framed as this:

Unless the vasanas, the inner attachments, are already present, the outer attachments cannot pull the mind, making it wander here and there, preventing it from getting established in Self-abidance. Therefore, those who possess the greatness of a stilled mind do not incur any blemish, irrespective of whatever environment they may reside in. The implication is: only inner attachment is truly attachment, outer attachment is not the problem. (GVK, V. 912).

So if spiritual practice is mature, if there is no inner attachment, if the mind is stilled, immune to being triggered from without, no blemish will incur, no rage will fly, no penalty from your side of the scrimmage. Then you can remain the force of love in marriage or any context. Then marriage can serve as a valuable proving ground and barometer of spiritual development. That is why I have shied away from providing couples therapy. In the long run, the work has to be one's own - in attaining a mind free from attachment.

My first formal meditation instruction was in the Soto tradition of Zen. In the Rinzai Zen tradition, I was told, a teacher with a stick monitors the room. If you move, you are struck (lovingly) with the stick. The practice is to sit without moving in reaction to whatever may arise - including restlessness and discomfort. You remain still, you maintain the frame, so as to fully contact, without moving away from whatever discomfort the body and mind cough up. This practice has implications for marriage. In the course of marriage many uncomfortable thoughts and feelings will be coughed to the surface: resentments, rage, restlessness, lust for another, the feeling there is greener grass elsewhere. Marriage as a practice requires that the frame is maintained without moving so that whatever comes up is dealt with. Because what does come up are inner attachments. If there is no inner capacity for anger, resentment, or lust - impurity of mind - then marriage can remain a context of deepening unconditional love. Changing the frame is an acquiescence to discomfort and, if there were a Zen master in the room, he would hit you with a stick, requiring that you remain unmoved, overcoming whatever inner discomfort or attachment is preventing the greatness of a stilled mind and a loving heart.

(I am not speaking of abusive or dangerous situations which, of course, should be abandoned in the interest of self care and protection).

Whatever mental state arises in the context of marriage (or any situation) is useful information because that mental state - say anger - is within you. You may not have known that you still had the capacity for that anger, but it arose because the vasanas (mental habits) have not been fully eradicated, and you are being shown the remaining residues that need to be purified.

Muscle Memory

Andy talked about God's Flesh - psilocybin mushrooms - and ayahuasca, drugs that may afford a glimpse of higher consciousness. But when you come down from the high you are pretty much where you were before you left, except for the glimpse into something not previously seen. Spiritual practice, on the other hand, develops the muscle memory of higher consciousness so that higher consciousness is internalized, in your bones, deeply familiar; it's where you live, not just a place you visit.

Performance

There are stories in the spiritual literature of epiphanies arising spontaneously - suddenly an awakening - and the world is seen afresh, but the freshness comes unexpectedly, without preparation, without grounding in theory, so there is no map, no context in which to place the experience. What just happened?

The experience fades, as all experience does, because you have no idea how to sustain it, what it means, where this experience fits into the overall scheme of the human journey. If the map were known, or if there were a well versed teacher to consult, the experience could be placed into context - oh, I have read about this, this location is well marked, should be interpreted thus, with practice can be sustained, a baseline from which even grander perspectives can grow. The map orients, as with driving across the country. You know from the map that it's three thousand miles from New York to San Francisco, how long it will take to drive, how much it will cost, what landscapes you will encounter, where each landscape fits into the whole. You know you will cross great plains and rocky mountains, but the grandeur of the Great Plains and Rocky Mountains will only be grasped once the journey is made. I once visited Joshua Tree National Park, got a map at the Visitor Center, knew from the map that there was a lookout ahead, but actually looking out over hundreds of miles of desert and mountains all the way to Palm Springs was not like the squiggle on the map. Still, without the squiggle, I would not have found my way to the place of awe.

Spiritual visionaries are the adventurers who draw the map in the first place. It is said that what separates the Buddha from an arhat, a fully enlightened disciple, is that the Buddha ventured first, discovered and pointed the way. Without his illumination the disciple - and humanity in general - would still be floundering. The arhat crosses to the same shore by virtue of the Buddha's instruction. The destination may be the same but the Buddha, like a spiritual Lewis and Clark, first sets out into the unknown to return with the map.

My friend, Jason, is an actor who writes and performs in theater. I asked whether he experiences a heightened state on stage. He answered," Yes, of course." We speculated that performers in all spheres of entertainment - actors, dancers, musicians, athletes - experience a heightened state of awareness on stage. But without understanding the place this heightened state holds in the greater scheme of the human journey, without the map, the state has no greater significance. An athlete may experience a heightened state from performing in a stadium holding sixty thousand people but may not live a good life, may afterwards get drunk or engage in violence. There may be no understanding that the heightened state has significance and can be sustained beyond the arena.

What does this signify? The heightened state is the timeless state and results from complete absorption in the present, a silencing of the mundane mind preoccupied with past and future. The heightened state can be sustained permanently if it is understood in the context of the human psyche, and if the muscle memory of heightened awareness is developed. This is the goal of spiritual practice, for the heightened state to become the default state. The goal of spiritual practice is to maintain the heightened state whether on God's Flesh, on stage or in the stadium, understanding that the joy of increased awareness should be held, is a compass needle pointing toward truth.

Theory and Practice

Sarah has a busy mind - always analyzing everything - and anxiety, a mind that cannot rest. She reads books to learn how to be free of anxiety and she meditates. But there are so many books and so many ways to meditate! Which is right? A popular meditation app includes thousands of meditations, and spiritual advice fills the bookshelves. Given her mind's propensities, the plethora of spiritual theory and practice offers just another target for over-analysis and confusion.

It is said the Buddha gave each person individualized meditation instructions. He knew each person's propensities and gave precise instructions to suit that person's temperament. In the confusing maze, some theory and practice will suit better than others. Let peace be the compass that points you toward truth.

Theory is the map, the intellectual understanding of the journey. Practice is the undertaking of the journey, actually hitting the road.

Mind Destruction

The website for an insurance company lists the different kinds of behavioral health treatments it offers. Among these is, "Mind expansion therapy." I think I will call the treatment I offer, "Mind destruction therapy." (Of course, when small M mind is destroyed, large M, expanded mind is revealed).

Distracted

I am often asked, "how can you function without thinking?" I reply, "Only when you are distracted by many thoughts do you miss your exit on the highway." The busyness of thinking is friction that interferes with smooth functioning. When the mind is not preoccupied, when attention is present and fully available, you effortlessly take the correct exit, and perform other work with equal efficiency and ease.

SEEM

SEEM: Sleeping, Eating, Exercise, Meditation (or Mind). I often refer to foundational practices in the SEEM acronym, four aspects of daily life that need to be disciplined and kept on track for health in body and mind.

Identity

Unsure of herself, having been reared in a non-affirming family, she assumed many personas so as to be liked in school. She was the musical girl who played the flute, the flute girl. She was the girl who brought brownies to class (for there was no surer path to approval than brownies), the brownie girl. But the personas were constructed for a purpose. Now older, the constructs were cumbersome and could no longer be maintained. She could not lie to herself or others, gaining approval for what she could produce. With no construct, what identity was left? Who am I without a constructed identity? The doorway to truth is opening. Who are you truly? See if you can touch your true identity, the unconstructed, authentic, the light behind all the constructed identities, the pure "I," the Self. And until you can, take on faith that there will be a happy ending, for the discovery of truth will certainly bring joy.

Trans

An adolescent, he wanted to begin the process of transitioning from male to female. He never felt like he fit in with the boys, was socially uncomfortable, and felt that with transition he would be more comfortable in his body. But was he uncomfortable in his body, so that changing his body would heal the problem, or was he uncomfortable in his mind and changing his body, like changing location, the geographical cure, was not addressing the root problem? He was anxious and socially uncomfortable, uncomfortable in his existence and who, if not spiritually mature, is comfortable in existence?

Perhaps that is where the problem should be addressed: what needed to heal was mind, to abandon mind, sink into heart, at which point the body might be seen as an irrelevance.

However, if your car has a flat tire, call AAA and get the flat repaired. I would not advise that you simply be at peace with a flat tire on the side of the road; be at peace while waiting for AAA to come. With transgender patients, if gender identity is truly the problem, perhaps the problem should be fixed. Do not attempt to be at peace while the problem remains at the level that the problem presents. But, again, is the problem at the level of the body or the mind? If the mind finds body parts unappealing, that could be a chicken thought. I don't like parts of my body; who hasn't had that thought? Perhaps, if the mind dies, so will the transgender problem - and all problems.

Transgender surgery will not end suffering. Transgender surgery will not yield enlightenment. Suffering is a function of the mind/ego and, ultimately, that is the amputation that needs to be performed.

Shame

Shame is a universal malady and most shame is about the body, some body part that is seen as imperfect. Thoughts of body-part-shame seem gripping, but the grip should be released to be free from this unnecessary, self inflicted pain.

Frustration

Frustration implies desire; frustration is the frustration of desire. If there is no desire, there can be no frustration.

After Muruganar

Grace is the cool water that calms the scorching heat of affliction in body and mind.

Mantras

A three word mantra for prosperity in form: Grace, Success, Wealth. Grace descends, that which cannot be controlled, the inexplicable stroke of good fortune, whether material - you win the lottery, you get into Harvard, you get the call from Oprah - or spiritual, the heart surges into blossoming, the stars line up and suddenly all is seen through the eyes of grace. Success arrives, the trudging along day to day ends, the doors to success open, like switching from a bullock cart to supersonic transport. And the outcome of Grace and Success is Wealth, the weight of life is removed, there is plenty, plenty for all your needs and dreams of generosity. Taste joy of liberation in the material realm.

Other mantras: Grace. A fish swims over to another fish and asks, "Have you ever seen the ocean?" The second fish replies, "I'm not sure, let's go ask that fish over there." So they swim to the third fish who says, "No I don't think I have but I heard that my great-grandfather saw the ocean." So they built a statue of the great-grandfather fish and worshipped him because he had seen the ocean.

We are always swimming in the ocean of grace. You are embedded in, surrounded by the ocean of grace. Recognize the Ever-Present ocean of grace. The Self is the ocean of grace.

Those who have realized the truth will abide firmly in that truth, realizing that there is no fault in creation, but only in one's view of it. (The Shining of My Lord, P. 48).

Perfection. Baruch Spinoza, the seventeenth century philosopher, proposed that the universe is God, God is perfect, so the universe is perfect at all times. This and every moment is God's perfection. Release the preoccupation of thought, of mind/ego that is rife with dilemma, recognize and rest in Ever-Present beauty and perfection.

Realm. In using the word, "realm," as a mantra, see this world as *a* realm, not the only realm. See this world as one realm among many possible realms. Look around at this world with interest, a curious place to have come, an opportunity to play by a particular set of rules, to learn the lessons this realm has to offer, then to depart. The "realm" perspective loosens the grip your situation might hold, seeing your situation as an interesting development in this, one temporary realm among many, which will serve the purposes of your soul before you move on to some other realm elsewhere.

Royalty. You are royalty, rest in your grandeur.

Feast. Life is a feast, the visual world is a sumptuous feast, imbibe the feast of life and beauty, rather than be preoccupied in dilemma.

Be love. Shawn came up with the mantra, "Be love," and it's a good mantra. I tried it yesterday myself to good effect. Today I look out to the lavish beauty of nature by which I am surrounded, and modify the mantra to, "Be *in* love," to allow myself to be thrilled by beauty, to bow low before that beauty in worship.

Bathe in Grace. One of my favorites. Allow yourself to bathe in the grace that is the nature of being. To what do you pay attention? Pay attention to grace.

The Emergence of Truth

Even during his days as a heroin addict he knew that he had a greater destiny. He couldn't just acquiesce to a fate of heroin. The pull toward something greater, something healthier, the pull to emerge from the lies, theft, and betrayals that the heroin lifestyle engendered propelled him beyond his addiction. Believe it or not, he has just completed his first year of law school, wants to work for social justice, now wears button down shirts and horn rimmed glasses. Like someone reaching for the surface while drowning, he felt the urgency to rise out of an environment of death, back to land where his lungs could breathe freely again. Like someone lost in a thicket with darkness descending, he pushed hard to find his way into the clearing. And he did. Pulled by truth, he cast off falsehood.

The impulse toward truth is universal. The soul wants to find its way out of bewilderment of all sorts, because bewilderment is always uncomfortable. The soul knows something is wrong and that something better is possible. Even if there is worldly success, the soul knows there is more to be done, more clarity to be realized. So the emergence of truth continues until truth overcomes all obstacles, until light chases away all darkness. The full emergence of truth - what can be called enlightenment - is the final recognition of what has always called for recognition, the most pervasive, obvious, and undeniable fact of being: I Am - pure, unsullied being, beyond any taint of impurity or limitation. The pull toward spiritual truth cannot be denied and, because nothing else will work in the long run, inevitably truth will emerge in a given life and in the life of the world.

All You Can Eat

I have learned that all you can eat buffets engender sickness through overeating, the false impression that food of every taste will bring happiness. On closer examination, excessive food brings malaise. I spoke with a libertarian, a supporter of the second amendment, and disagreed with his belief that guns are a great bounty. I believe the second amendment is obsolete, produces a uniquely American sickness of gun violence that, on closer investigation, brings death and sorrow. The "right" to guns is death cloaked in the appearance of benevolence. The prevalence of media in our society is perhaps a new sickness. Like the buffet, it appears free access to screens and their abundant information is a bounty. But constant information, like an invasive species, overruns the mind, supplanting stillness and peace.

Therapy

Psychodynamic therapies tend to address content, especially the content of a person's history which is explored for the root of maladaptive conditioning.

When you have a cluttered room and remove the clutter from the room, the room appears spacious. The space was there all along, just obscured by the clutter.

In the process of meditation, the mind coughs up its contents and they disperse. This is what Thomas Keating has called "the unloading of the unconscious." As the unconscious is unloaded there is more space. The space was there all along, just obscured by the clutter.

Psychology tends to focus on the figure, not the ground. Psychology tends to focus on the contents of the unconscious, not the space that contains it. That space is consciousness, the being within which the contents of mind are contained. So the progression into the spiritual can also be considered the progression from figure to ground, from the content of mind (figure) to the space within which the content is contained (ground), now purified of content.

The contents of mind are problems; the contours of ego. The space that remains when consciousness is purified of its contents (mind), present all along but obscured by the clutter, is pure being, Eternal Being, true nature, the Self, happiness.

Fairy Tales

Fairy tales represent the soul's knowledge that liberation awaits - when you find the prince or princess of your dreams, retire to a magic castle, and live *happily ever after*. A pot of gold at the end of the rainbow. The liberation that the soul seeks, projected as the fairy tale, is more likely Nirvana, the true pot of gold, liberation not to a fanciful castle where the prince and princess probably end up in couples therapy or fighting over custody, but permanent liberation of the mind/ego into heart and Ever-Presence.

Electric Fan

A fan, when unplugged, loses its current and vitality. Now, unplug the mind, remove its current and vitality, allow its movement to slow to a halt. The mind, like the unplugged fan, is now silent and peace, which the movement obscured, can be tasted. Tasting the peace of silence requires de-energizing the mind, electrified by outer-ness.

Where Thoughts and Stories End

10. Verses on Truth

The Paradox of Truth

Only the fullness that lacks for nothing in all times and in all places is the truth. (GVK, P. 34).

Truth is, by definition, ever present. Truth is the eternal, another name for God. It is never not truth; it is never not eternity; it is never not God. Like hydrogen in the universe, truth is the most common and boundless element. Yet truth - the fullness that lacks for nothing - is also exquisitely beautiful, like a precious gem or the painting of a master. Usually objects of exquisite beauty are very rare and therefore costly. The paradox of truth: the most abundant substance is also the most precious.

The Paradox of Eternity

As you approach what is most intimate, you approach the eternal.

True North

The Oxford Dictionaries chose "post-truth" as word-of-the-year for 2016. We live in a "post-truth" era where truth is an outdated notion from a quaint past. But to some, an era where truth is obsolete has no interest, because only truth is worthy of interest. So those who are alienated from an era that is "post-truth" may feel themselves going "post-world."

A world where truth is obsolete is ripe for spiritual teaching from the "post-world" contingent. Because those who are beyond the drama of the world, whose gaze is fixed on True North and cannot be swayed, their worldliness drowned in the passion for transcendence, who cannot be enticed by the false promises of impermanence, who are firmly anchored in and so embody truth, are in the best position to remind the world what it has forgotten. A world that has lost truth has lost its bearings. Spiritual teaching has always been a ray of light from the North Star, a reminder of True North, so that the "post-truth" world may regain its compass, and be once more oriented toward the radiance - of truth, of the heart - that unfailingly points the way towards love.

Holding

Having been lost at sea in a storm without bearings, not knowing which direction is east, west, north, or south, the clouds finally part to reveal the North Star. The ship is now oriented, the direction is clear. The storm is the mind; the North Star is the heart. Hold to the heart, unwavering "I-ness" which leads one out of turmoil. Hold to the truth/heart; do not be distracted into falsehood/mind.

Monkey Trap

Jack Kornfield told the story of the monkey trap in Thailand. A hole is carved in a coconut and a sweet placed inside the coconut. The hole is large enough for the monkey to insert its hand, but not large enough for the monkey to remove its fist once the sweet is grasped. With a coconut hanging from its arm, the monkey is easily captured. All the monkey needs to do to escape is to release its grasp on the sweet, and the coconut will fall from its hand. The monkey's grasping insures its capture.

Life is a dream and it is only our desire toward the dream that keeps it a going concern. Without grasping toward the dream, the dream has no psychological charge. It is the expectation of finding happiness within, creating a dream to our liking, that maintains involvement in the dream. Without this expectation, without taking the dream seriously, with detachment, the dream becomes an amusement.

If the end of grasping ends involvement in the dream, then releasing desire is emancipation. Releasing involvement in the dream requires releasing preoccupation with anything that is not truth, and so requires a dedication to truth at the expense of involvement in thoughts of desire, and the expectation of finding fulfillment from within the dream.

The internet is rife with opinions from those taking the dream seriously. I believe that those who are beyond the dream should be consulted regarding the politics of the dream.

Veritas

I attended an alumni talk by Drew Faust, the president of Harvard University, who was understandably extolling the virtues of the university, its spirit of exploration in all the arts and sciences. I was inspired by the talk to write to the Dean of the Divinity School to ask if I could teach a course at the school. I realized during the talk that, while the motto of the university is Veritas - truth - the university looks for truth in only one direction. All the disciplines in the university look through a lens to study the world. But nowhere in the university does the lens turn backward so that the looker looks at the looker who is looking, so that the subject who is looking becomes the object of inquiry. While the university may investigate in many directions, it does not investigate the source of investigation.

I heard the idea recently that this world may just be a simulation. In other words, this world may not be real, it's a simulation within some grander context that contains and has constructed the simulation, it's the Matrix, one optional location in infinite consciousness composed of many possible locations, one appearance that will morph at some point into another kind of appearance.

If that is the case then the university is studying the characteristics of this simulation and how important is that? If you have a dream at night and, within the dream, are studying the properties of the dream, say, the properties of dream air and the mechanics of dream flying in dream air, how important when you wake up are the mechanics of dream flying? Do the mechanics diligently studied within the dream extend beyond the dream? Will all the arts and sciences studied diligently within the university, about which so many articles are written, have any bearing once we leave here? In one hundred years, how important will American history, earth science, or evolutionary psychology be to anyone now reading these words?

So if this world is a simulation, one locus in a multiverse of infinite loci, how important in the greater scheme are the properties of this simulation? If, upon death, we leave here to visit another simulation, call it heaven, how important will the properties of this simulation be in the next? Here gravity rules but maybe everyone flies all over the place in heaven! What would be important to know, then, are the truths that apply here and are carried over to the next simulation, and the next. That we could actually call truth because it is always true, true in every simulation, true in all times and in all places. The truth must be true throughout the multiverse, holding through all simulations, and so is as true now as it will ever be, because the truth is always true. So what is it that is always true, as true now as it would be in any other simulation? What is always the case, what never wavers in this life or the next? The seer, seeing itself, the origin of investigation, I Am, consciousness, being, eternity. You, as the light of being, were in the dream state, you are here in the waking state, you will be in heaven, you will be regardless of the extraneous properties of the realm in which you find yourself. Because what you truly are is Eternal Being and Eternal Being is always the case, that which allows all simulations to be. Funny that Eternal Being is the one thing omitted from study in a university with the motto of Veritas. For the Dean never responded to my letter.

The Pearl Beyond Price

A student of Walt Whitman, he disagreed with my proposal that love is inevitable in the personal and social sphere. He preferred to think that love is a brave choice in a corrupt world where selfishness often rules. But love is inevitable, I believe, because any choice other than love is equivalent to suffering. Any choice other than love will fail because it is inconsistent with the nature of the soul. The organism knows what suits it, its compass steers toward truth via the outcome of happiness, and only truth will yield happiness in the long run. What makes the organism ill - falsehood, non-love - will eventually be rejected.

If you eat unwholesome food the organism becomes ill. Unwholesome food by definition does not suit the organism and has a bad taste. If food is rotten it tastes bad. If you are foraging, you are looking for food that suits by taste. The taste tells whether the food suits the organism or not.

If, internally, you move in directions away from the heart, the organism will similarly inform that happiness is decreasing. So movement toward the heart, toward truth, is inevitable because nothing else works; nothing else will bring about the happiness you seek. And the search for happiness never wanes; the souls deepest, ever present longing. Until that longing is fulfilled in truth the search will continue.

The treasure hunt yields success, the treasure is found, truth: nothing is more precious. Shanti, Shanti, Shanti. The taste of truth is joy. The pearl beyond price has been found.

What I Did Not Learn from Buddhism

The three characteristics of experience according to Buddhism are anicca, anatta, and dukkha. All experience is impermanent, without self, and unsatisfactory.

One of Ramana Maharshi's metaphors: when a movie appears on a screen, while the movie may change, the screen is unchanging and permanent.

The three characteristics of experience according to Buddhism are characteristics of the movie, not of the screen. What I did not learn from Buddhism: to focus on and recognize the characteristics of the screen, not the movie. The screen is eternal and unchanging; the substratum or source of the impermanent.

While Buddhism may allude to the eternal as Nirvana, in my experience, it is not emphasized. What *is* emphasized is observation of the impermanent nature of experience and the recognition that impermanence can never be truly satisfying. True; so where is satisfaction to be found? And who is observing; what is the source of the observation? With this inquiry the focus shifts from observing phenomena to abiding as the observer. The focus shifts from the impermanent to the permanent source of which the impermanent is a manifestation.

When meditating according to Buddhist lights, the observer notices the impermanent and unsatisfying characteristics of experience. When meditating according to the lights of non-dualism, the permanent and satisfying substratum of experience is recognized. And the characteristics of the substratum, consciousness, are opposite, that is, the screen is the permanent, eternal Self, the heart, home, and its nature is not suffering but abundant peace.

I have heard it said that, according to Buddhism, since everything is impermanent, consciousness is also impermanent. If that is the case then how can you know that consciousness is impermanent? Because if consciousness flickers on and off, how would you know? There would be no underlying awareness to recognize the flickering. The flickering of impermanence is recognized only because it flickers against an unchanging backdrop and that backdrop is the eye of awareness that sees all.

Insight

I can be inspired by truth or by beauty.
To write truth is to write insight,
to write beauty is to write poetry,
this itself an insight,
this writing the writing of insight,
in the form of poetry.

Never Not God

Western mystics have aspired to attain union with God. It is truer to say that union with God is always the case. It is never not God. Union with God is the ever present state.

Supreme Value

The supreme value is to be valued above all other values because only the supreme value can end want forever. How can there be want when in possession of the supreme value: truth, the fullness that lacks for nothing?

Travel

Travel is stimulating, a way to experience diversity in geography and culture. Travel involves moving the body. Meditation involves moving the body not at all, the suspension of bodily movement, so that all travel, all movement and exploration takes place inwardly, in mind and consciousness alone.

Kant

It is said of Immanuel Kant, considered the greatest modern philosopher in the west, that people could know the time by his movements. He would cross the town square at the same time each day. While his life displayed little outer movement, inwardly he was in great movement and produced a monumental body of work.

Ramana Maharshi left home at sixteen for the mountain of Arunachala in South India and, for the rest his life, never left. While travel can expand horizons, for some it is simpler to minimize bustle, keeping the outer frame stable, so that depth of journeying is done primarily within.

Blessed

To feel blessed it is not enough to *be* blessed - with material wealth, with meaningful work, with loving family - for one could be in that midst and still feel impeded by mind and desire, by wanting something different. The state of blessing requires gratitude, for no abundance in circumstances can confer the *experience* of blessing, which is that gratitude and nothing more, regardless of circumstances.

Location

Nicolae Tanase invited me to contribute to his website, Excellence Reporter, which asks artists, writers, spiritual figures their answer to the question, "What is the meaning of life?" After sending my answer along, I asked Nicolae if we could have lunch sometime, where was he located? I realized that the question was ambiguous. I was asking, of course, where could I meet him for lunch, where on the planet would Google maps zoom in to pinpoint his location? But on another level, where is anyone located? Do you have location at all? If you are consciousness and not a body, nothing specific, then how can the non-specific be located? Truer to say you are nowhere and everywhere - they mean the same thing - not a location Google can pinpoint on a map.

Holy of Holies

Located at the heart of the temple in ancient Jerusalem was the Holy of Holies, the inner sanctum, the sacred chamber, which was entered only by the high priest on Yom Kippur. The holiest place entered at the holiest time by the holiest of men. The temple's Holy of Holies is an architectural representation of the true Holy of Holies located within, the place of utmost purity, the innermost flame of the radiant heart. Entering the Holy of Holies requires concentration, so that mind eschews distraction into everything mundane, so that mind touches its essence.

The Meaning of Life

My response to Nicolae.

The Meaning of Life: God is never distant, absent, or other.

As a ray of light shined through a prism diffracts into a spectrum of color, the Eternal Light, when shined through the body, diffracts into the spectrum of the five senses and world perception.

The purpose of life is to abide as the Eternal Light which, when shined through the body, projects the world. However, when the Eternal Light identifies with the body through which it shines it becomes an ego, mis-taking itself to be that distinct body/mind through which it shines, separate from the world which it perceives as outside and other, as if the perceived world and its actors were not themselves projections of the Eternal Light.

The ego, the separate entity which goes by the name you are called, then becomes involved in its stories, the drama of life, the drama of desire directed toward objects of the world. To abide as the Eternal Light - this is the process of spiritual awakening - attention must be withdrawn from preoccupation with the temporal story lines of desire that comprise the mind and ego. Attention comes to rest in its source and fundamental nature as the Eternal Light. Then it can truly be said that, "God is never distant, absent, or other." God is all there is; All God All the Time; it is Never Not God.

The mind is the locus of preoccupation with the world and thus the locus of suffering. What remains when the mind, ego, and suffering are abandoned into the purity of stillness? Joy and delight in the beauty of the Eternal Light and its manifestations. But this joy arises, again, with stillness of mind. Stillness requires a renunciation of everything that is not the Eternal Light, and so amounts to supreme devotion to truth, at the expense of worldliness and illusion. When the mind is purified of all content only the Eternal Light remains.

How do we know that this is the purpose of life? Because, while preoccupied with the world and desire directed toward the world, there is a feeling of unease. Something feels out of sorts. I am seeking something that the world of impermanence never can provide. The feeling of unease abates when the natural condition - what in the East is called *sahaja* - is restored. In the natural condition the feeling of unease, of being out of sorts is finally relieved. I have returned home. Like a carpenter's level, the bubble is finally aligned perfectly to center, to the heart. Anything other than home - the heart, the natural condition, sahaja - will feel off; incomplete and unsatisfactory.

The meaning of life, then, is not something that I know as an object, it is experiential. I *am* the meaning of life. And the paradox is that this meaning is both entirely at hand, as close and self evident as existence itself, and entirely transcendent in being pristine, beyond all content. I am, and I am beyond all particulars. Not this particular body/mind that arises at this particular time in this particular world appearance. Not the details of this particular movie, but something transcendent and absolute: I am emptiness and fullness, nothing and everything, boundless, timeless, and yet as close as close can be, as close as this moment, as intimate as this moment and yet vast, for when the mind is *empty* of stories, nothing remains to obstruct the natural state of the heart which is completely *full*... with love.

For love is the nature of the brimming heart. Anything other than love, the brimming heart, feels lacking and we will be compelled to correct, to realign to love, where the journey, joyfully recognizes its culmination.

War and Peace

What do you want to experience throughout eternity? Peace, the absence of war which means: not being at war with yourself.

Taste God

Stop long enough to taste the present moment, which is to say… taste God.

Conflagration

The vision of this excellent effulgence is similar to the sight of an unbounded conflagration that rages when a vast forest, dense with dried trees, catches fire and spreads in all directions. GVK, V. 1011.

The heart is a furnace, a roaring furnace, that spews BTU's of love and well-being.

The Heart and the All

Wisdom tells me I am nothing. Love tells me I am everything. Between these two my life flows - Nisargadatta

In BSB the Self was defined as "the Heart and the All." Two metaphors were used to illustrate "the Heart and the All" which can be applied to this famous quote from Nisargadatta.

The heart was illustrated using the metaphor of a target, an archery target, with rings surrounding the bull's eye, each farther-out ring at another level of remove from the bull's eye. (Here the bull's eye is the heart. In the tree metaphor, the trunk is the heart, with branches extending farther and farther away from the heart, like rings from the bull's eye). Wisdom is the attempt to get at truth, the truth of what I am, the most substantial truth, not the outer rings but the very core. To get at the heart I look past the superficial to arrive at the substantial. Where is the heart of my being, what is actually substantial? Where can I rest in peace, having come home to the sacred? So I negate what is not truth, what is not substantial. I look to the world and notice that everything I perceive is fleeting; everything comes and goes. Consistent with Buddhist teaching, all objects of perception are impermanent, including perception of body and mind. What *is* substantial is the perceiver, the subject who persists through all the changes. I am not anything that I perceive as a fleeting object, rather *I am perception itself.* Wisdom tells me I am nothing. I am nothing I can put my finger on or, if I can put my finger on it, *that ain't it*. The heart, the truth is closer, more intimate than anything I can know as an object. *I am knowing itself*, Being/Consciousness, the knowing that persists unchanged through all changes in insubstantial objects of perception.

But *knowing*, like space, is vast, without boundary. And everything that I perceive - the world - arises within this knowing; nothing is outside or apart. The metaphor in BSB for vastness - the All - was Russian Dolls. In the metaphor of the target, truth is at the center with rings extending outward. Reversing this idea, in the Russian Doll metaphor, truth is the largest doll that contains everything, with lesser phenomena contained within. Love tells me I am everything. The vast space of consciousness embraces everything without preference or judgment; everything is held within its embrace. When I arrive at my heart through negation, when I can no longer say that I am anything in particular, I realize that I am everything in general. There is nothing that is not contained within my being. So truth is simultaneously the Heart and the All, Wisdom and Love, Negation and Inclusion, Nothing and Everything, the very center that yet has no boundary, no beginning or end. The most intimate Heart is simultaneously the vastness of All; Endlessness.

The world is an illusion. Brahman alone is real. Brahman is the world.

This classic formula, which Ramana quoted, makes the same point. I begin my search for truth with negation. I negate the world as an impermanent, unsatisfactory illusion. I am searching for truth and only the eternal - Brahman, God - will satisfy. I reject the impermanent to arrive at the permanent. Having done so, having come to the heart, having settled upon the eternal, I realize that *All* is the eternal for the eternal can have no boundary, no demarcation that states: "this is outside or other than the eternal." Brahman alone is real - but Brahman is the world; the world which at first I rejected as illusion is also, and not other than, That.

Ancient

That which is most ancient is that which is most intimately present.

QED

Heart = All
but
Heart = Source
and
All = Endlessness
so
Source = Endlessness
or
Atman = Brahman

quod erat demonstrandum

11. Verses on Beauty

The Left Bank

When I was twenty years old, I hitchhiked across Europe. I was fond of reading Hemingway, remember liking his spare, minimalist style and existentialist sense, the fraught situations and emotions of characters caught in the human condition. He would sit in the cafés of Europe writing stories and, as I explored the Plaka in Athens, dreamed that I too would someday sit in bustling cafés, in exotic locations, listening to the lilt of Romance languages, pen in hand, ideas flowing onto paper.

Today I am waiting for my car while it gets light body work. I find a bagel joint where I wait for the call on my cell from the shop that the car is ready. I am sitting outside, in the shade beneath the overhang of a balcony, on a hot, ninety degree July morning. Some teachings in the New Age genre believe that the universe manifests dreams. It's been forty five years but here I am, not in the Plaka or Barcelona or the Left Bank, but in Central Massachusetts with a laptop not a pen, a bagel not a baguette, the lilting conversations around me punctuated only with the usual Boston inflected English but, in a strange way, my dream has come to pass.

Creative

Listening to the Beatles station on satellite radio, I saw the progression from one phase to the next phase in their creative process and how that process never abated. Once one album representing one phase was complete, the next album and phase would begin, with enormous growth during their years together. This illustrates the life of the creative, continually channeling one moment's creativity, then the next moment's creativity, never resting on the accomplishments of the past, but allowing the river to keep flowing, to venture into ever new and fresh territories of the unconscious, writing one song or chapter then another, thus leaving a growing oeuvre behind. Therapy is creative but leaves no recording and so no larger impact beyond the effects of that day's interaction. In writing as in music, however, creativity is documented so that a legacy remains that can endure beyond the moment of inspiration.

Stream of Consciousness

Stream of consciousness is one art form,
versus the perfectly crafted verse,
each word chosen to perfection.
In stream of consciousness, however,
can each word be chosen to perfection?
If attunement to the moment is perfect,
will each word in the stream be perfect,
saying exactly what that moment wants to say,
as perfect as the sky and sun,
unerring in their eternal stream of poetry?

Faith

While meditating as a monk in Burma, I was told by the elder monks that the Burmese made more rapid progress in meditation than the Westerners because the indigenous Burmese venerated their teachers and did exactly as they were instructed. Trusting the guru and following his guidance, rapid progress was made. Not so for Westerners for whom everything was just so complicated. In my own practice I speak with many patients who would do well just to follow the instructions they are given, but instead argue. The directions are sound and would lead them swiftly to their destination, but the ego must have its way. So, when warranted, when the teacher is expert in the lay of the land, it is best to trust and to follow the teacher's directions on faith.

Graduation

My daughter graduated with her Masters degree from Columbia University in New York. The day was wet, cold for May, and she wore her graduation gown as an extra layer as we walked downtown to the restaurant to celebrate. People passing by expressed congratulations to the graduate on the Manhattan sidewalks. On that chilly day, those simple gestures of good will provided very welcome warmth.

Comfort Zone

There is an often declared value to living outside of one's comfort zone. In a way, I want to go further *into* my comfort zone, into the sense of being internally comfortable, more and more at peace, more and more at home within my Self. Ramana Maharshi, who lived in South India, used the example of cool shade to represent the Self. Why would you leave the cool shade to scurry around in the scorching heat of Samsara? Remain at home, in the heart, where all is exceedingly comfortable. Go deeper into the heart, the place of ultimate comfort.

Moss

Have you smelled moss lately? We live in a shade forest where moth grows prodigiously and forms a natural carpet for yoga. I was on my knees twirling the moss and, sadly, some pulled from the earth. So that its life might not be in vain, I held the moss to my nostrils and inhaled, and inhaled deeply again. The perfume of earth is distilled into moss, earth speaks as scent in the scent of moss, the robust essence of earth in so delicate a form.

Weather

Yesterday, February in New England , there were near blizzard conditions. The snow was blowing mightily; outside the picture window currents of swirling white powder obscured the view even of the trees just beyond the glass. Today the skies are clear, the air is quiet. The first spring birds are making their voices heard.

Weather is a good metaphor for life. Conditions are always changing and in flux. I may prefer when it's eighty and sunny and sometimes those conditions are met. Sometimes it actually is eighty and sunny! But inevitably change comes. When it gets hotter than eighty, the summer skies become gray and overcast, the temperature soars with tropical downpours to follow. When it's very cold, as in winter last year, the entire peach crop in the northeast was destroyed on one brutally frigid day.

If I require eighty and sunny to be happy I will be disappointed most of the time. Unless I am able to achieve eighty and sunny *internally*. Then it is always eighty and sunny because *I* am eighty and sunny. Life sparkles wherever I gaze. The conditions are perfect. The blizzard, the downpours, all the wonders of weather are radiant, illuminated by the radiance of the seeing itself.

Window

I have worked in a small office for many years. Three of the office walls are interior, but one wall faces outside. There is a square window on this wall. The window overlooks a parking lot and, beyond the parking lot, a large tract of forest lies. Because of the open space, the parking lot just outside the window, there is a clear view to the sky. Because majestic trees line the far side of the parking lot, the sky is framed below with foliage.

Looking from this small office out this window is like looking at a flat screen TV hanging on the wall. But the program that appears on this screen is nature in motion. It is August, and the program playing today was the summer sky, gray and overcast, with afternoon downpours followed by clearing, resurgence, and a bright setting sun. On most days when the sky is clear, the blue radiance of the sky is backdrop to light shimmering like crystal on each of a thousand swaying leaves. Soon the pastel palette of autumn will arrive, the leaves will be turning, falling, to be followed by the sacred, silent snowfall wiping the landscape clean and cold. I am often the last one left in the building while the white silence descends.

Over the years, from inside this room, I have watched the changing scenery. I may sit with someone and together we watch the changing display outside the window. While the display may change, the seer who looks from inside the room - from inside the body inside the room - does not change. The seer is Eternal Being looking out at changing appearances, the dream of Eternal Being.

Breeze and Branch

The branches reaching upward,
reaching as worship,
reaching as devotion to their beloved,
in the forms of sky and sun,
cry love.
Trees are crying heavenward,
"O beloved, I reach to you with pure love,
this reaching an expression of my soul's desire."

And the heavens in turn embrace,
make space for every movement of devotion,
while the trees dance and sway, caressed by breezes,
dancing a dance of breeze and branch in mutual caress,
a world crying out in love.
And my heart too wants to join this dance of the divine,
to see the sublime wherever I turn.

Ode to November

Many in New England say they dislike November, not the autumnal glory and still-warm weather of October, not the white grace dusting of winter soon to come. Yet November is a color all its own in the spectrum of seasons; alright, not the technicolor of October, more like a glowing yellow luminescence, with temperatures that still support lounging outside in the leaf tannery, where yellow leaves are burnished by cold into leather. Ode to November, the forgotten month, bridge from fall to winter, with colors of both seasons blended on nature's palette.

What Bird Dares

One lone bird lingers late this season,
not intimidated by the onset of cold.

What bird stays with winter here,
a year round resident for sure?
What bird dares make its home in trees laid bare,

by the revolution of earth around sun,
leaving rays just warm enough for life's survival,
not the barren cold of Mars,
 just the cold of a dormant Earth?

What bird dares brave branches bared,
by the departure of leaves -
believe me, in the forest, blowing leaves off the lawn,
back into the forest,
is like pushing ocean away from shore!
What bird dares remain here days the sun sets,
when the day's barely begun?
What bird dares brave winter while wiser flocks fly to warmth?
What bird dares brave this sky unburdened of clouds,
allowing Earth's heat to escape into unappreciating space,
braving the raining down of leaves in a veritable leaf blizzard,
braving the cold wind
which chills my gloveless hands as I type,
this northern form of grace,
the grace of cold bite to the air?

As a child I played on the streets of Manhattan,
so bundled I could barely move
while constructing my snowman,
even in Washington Heights the white grace fell,
restoring innocence to the concrete,
nature overshadowing even the concrete,
and even there birds dared sit on window sills,
where coins were tossed to buskers singing in courtyards.

I wanted to sing myself but my father objected:

what will he be, a klezmer?
The conditions not right for a musical fate this lifetime,
I sit watching daring birds,
and write what music I can with words,
will pick the instruments back up in the latter days of life,
when winter comes and the only redemptive spring,
will be the spring of death,
warmed up in a new climate altogether.

Retirement

I remained befuddled, imagining I had compulsory duties to perform. My Guru then freed me completely from this sense of obligation through the experience of firm *jnana*, the state of oneness that is free from the bewilderment of the ego which brings into being the idea of mandatory duties. (The Shining of my Lord, P. 98).

I have work to do before I die. I have to finish this book and others. I would like to contribute guidance for those who seek, to counteract our age of political darkness, and to write for the pleasure of the craft. There is more work to do: I have to pay off the mortgage, help secure the children financially and in their life paths. But the state of peace is the cessation of work, stopping, tasting stillness, non-doing, the suspension of doing, retirement in a psychological sense or, if continuing to work, doing so without attachment, so that the work exudes from stillness, and the heart is retained whether work goes on or not.

Plato

During a college seminar on Plato, the professor noted that the Republic was considered a dialogue written later in Plato's career because, when a man is young, he tends to be concerned with metaphysics and grand purposes, whereas mature men become practical and concerned with affairs of the state.

In India the stages of life continue to progress. After Dharma, the stage of maturity - adulthood, duty, working, raising a family, involvement in social governance - one enters the final stage, Moksha, the stage of renunciation. Having fulfilled one's social responsibilities, all is renounced in the final quest for liberation. In the West, this amounts to retirement but, rather than play golf, in India one seeks God. As I enter that stage myself, I would tell my philosophy professor that a man's interest comes full circle. While in youth he may have been concerned with matters of meaning, eventually outgrowing starry eyed innocence to mature into adulthood when he bears the burden of social responsibility, in the final stage, the embrace of death growing warmer, he sets his sights firmly on the eternal, metaphysical once again, outgrows the mundane to become lost in the transcendent, to be drowned forever in the infinite.

The Ages of Life

When I was a young man in the age of Kama,
I saw beauty in the form of women,
dazzling incarnations of the goddess.
In mid-life in the age of Dharma,

I saw beauty in the form of nature and of my children.
As an old man in the age of Moksha,
(the body anyway),
I see beauty in the form of existence.
Outer beauty is no longer required,
objects are no longer required,
form is no longer required.
Beauty is what is and requires no experience,
no exotic destination,
no breathtaking sunset,
no set of benevolent circumstances,
no particular something to behold.
Existence is itself beauty,
and when existence is beauty,
when everything is seen with the eye of beauty,
then beauty is everywhere.
And if there is no beautiful something to behold,
even if there is nothing to behold at all,
well, that too would be beautiful.

Writing as Spiritual Practice

To write truth I must first locate truth, so in looking within for what wants to be written, I must first touch that place which is worth writing about. Writing as spiritual practice: requiring that the truth worth writing about is first touched within.

Prophesy

The world is the mind. The mind is the world. In other words, involvement in the world is involvement in thoughts about the world. If there are no thoughts about the world, no ego speaking to itself about the things of the world, what would remain is the silence of mere presence. Presence has no definition or boundary. Its taste is wonderment - or any of a thousand other tastes of delight. But all the thousand tastes belong to a single I, a single Aham. I, Aham, is the name of presence.

The world is the mind. The mind is the world. If there are no thoughts about the world, no ego speaking to itself about the things of the world, what would remain is the body extended without limit as the appearance of the world. But without desire and fear, gain and loss, wealth and poverty, getting or not getting what you want. In the absence of thoughts about the world what remains is I, Aham existing as all things.

The world is comprised of thoughts about the world. If there are no thoughts about the world, what remains? If there is no engagement in any thought pertaining to your participation in the world, no rehearsing of any of the scenarios that comprise your participation in the world, what remains? If thought does not venture from its home in the heart what remains is the purity of Aham as that which alone exists as everything.

Take dictation from the gods. But *I* hear the voices of the gods, the voices of the gods are in me, not separate, because all things are in me, because all things *are* me, there is no separate me to whom all this appears.

Take dictation from the gods, from the soul, for the voices of the gods and the soul are the same. Take dictation from the inner fount of beauty.

Winter is strong this year but her power is waning. Now February, winter's days are numbered. Though she may yet issue another blast of fire, the fiery cold of arctic ice, she may choose instead to smile gently and allow the birds to return, the hint of warmth to waft that little bit sooner. O February, what fate do you hold, fire and ice, or the gentle smile of an early spring, that little bit of grace descending, before the cold is finally chased away as spring matures and blossoms fully into the flowering, into the full fragrance of the flowering, the fully ripe, fully mature bosom of the flowering?

While dictation may be taken from the voice of the unconscious, the dictation I would take is not from the unconscious but from the source of the unconscious, and for the purposes of prophesy, to give voice to the primal voice of prophesy, communicating what most wants to be communicated, messages from the soul, for all messages are soul messages when speaking from Aham.

Prophesy says: God alone is, all is God, all is grace, release the grip of fear, fall into the sea of grace, drown in the sea of grace, for what greater prophesy could there be than to say: drown in the sea of happiness.

To speak from Aham is to take dictation from that which has always been, the heart of what you are, so what you are at heart has always been. Taking dictation from that which has always been is giving voice to the voice of prophesy.

Truth, Beauty, Love

If Truth and Beauty - the male and female principles - represent the first emergence upon the cleaving of the One, Love is the unifying force that compels Truth toward Beauty and Beauty toward Truth, in primal embrace wherein the cleaving is healed; with Truth and Beauty merging back into their original state of oneness.

If all colors are made out of three primary colors, the three primary principles out of which the universe is made are, perhaps, the principles of Truth, Beauty - and the unifying principle of Love.

Non-Dual

remove the thought: *this is **not** God*
then
this ***is*** God
All God All the Time
It is Never Not God
God is Never Distant, Absent, or Other

Where Thoughts and Stories End

Benediction

may you be granted every happiness
in the presence of the Infinite Grace
Love reunites all diffraction
into the original place
of Eternal Light

References

Dawidowicz, Lucy. The War Against the Jews. Bantam, 1976.

Maharshi, Ramana. Talks with Ramana Maharshi: On Realizing Abiding Peace and Happiness. Inner Directions, 2000.

Muruganar. Guru Vachaka Kovai. Translated by T.V. Venkatasubramanian, Robert Butler, and David Godman. David Godman/Avadhuta Foundation, 2008.

Muruganar. Padamalai. Translated by T.V. Venkatasubramanian, Robert Butler, and David Godman. David Godman/Avadhuta Foundation, 2005.

Muruganar. The Shining of My Lord. Translated by T.V. Venkatasubramanian and David Godman. David Godman/Avadhuta Foundation, 2017.

About the Author

A child of Holocaust survivors, Solomon Katz was fluent in the Jewish tradition and biblical Hebrew at an early age. He studied philosophy in college and afterwards joined the Lindisfarne spiritual community where he was introduced to Zen and Vipassana meditation. His interest in meditation led him to Asia where he lived as a Theravada Buddhist monk in Myanmar and Sri Lanka. By the time he returned home and began doctoral studies, he had spent three years in periods of silent meditation retreat. At Harvard University he earned concurrent graduate degrees in world religion and psychology. He trained in, practiced, and taught psychology at Mt. Auburn Hospital, a Harvard affiliated teaching hospital, and held a clinical faculty position at Harvard Medical School. He is the author of "Beauty as a State of Being," winner of multiple book awards, and lives in Harvard, Massachusetts where, while working as a psychologist, he and his wife raised a family of four beautiful girls, many animals, and many fruit trees planted over the years at which he loves to gaze, often with the teachings of Ramana Maharshi and Muruganar in hand.

Where Thoughts and Stories End

www.ingramcontent.com/pod-product-compliance
Lightning Source LLC
Chambersburg PA
CBHW061647040426
42446CB00010B/1624